**NEW HAMPSHIRE**
GEOGRAPHIC SERIES

NUMBER ONE

# New Hampshire

## PORTRAIT OF THE LAND AND ITS PEOPLE

by William G. Scheller

© 1988 American Geographic Publishing
Helena, Montana

William A. Cordingley, Chairman
Rick Graetz, Publisher
Mark Thompson, Director of Publications
Barbara Fifer, Assistant Book Editor

For David, who has yet to hear the loons.

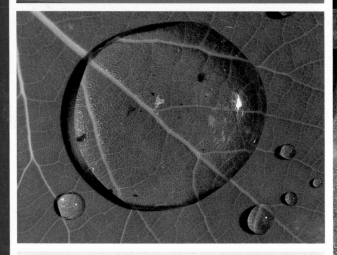

**Library of Congress Cataloging-in-Publication Data**

Scheller, William.
   New Hampshire : portrait of the land and its people / by William G. Scheller.
      p.   cm. — (New Hampshire geographic series ; no. 1)
     ISBN 0-938314-43-2 (pbk.) : $15.95
     1. New Hampshire—Description and travel.    I. Title. II. Series.
F34.S34 1988
974.2—dc 19

88-6070

ISBN 0-938314-43-2

© 1988 American Geographic Publishing
Box 5630, Helena, MT 59604
(406) 443-2842
Text © 1988 William G. Scheller
Design by Linda Collins.
Printed in Hong Kong by DNP America, Inc., San Francisco.

Just specimens is all New
Hampshire has,
One each of everything
as in a showcase,
Which naturally she
doesn't care to sell.
—Robert Frost
"New Hampshire"
1923

From *The Poetry of Robert Frost*, edited by Edward Connery Lathem, © 1979, Henry Holt and Company, Inc.

I would like to thank those individuals who assisted in the research and editing of this book, including John and Debbie Mahan, Richard Cushing, Guy Gosselin, Betsy McCoy, Peter Crane, William Copeley, Susan Bjørner, Barbara Fifer, Mark Thompson, the two anonymous characters in the Littleton Diner, and my Pittsburg fishing guide.

William G. Scheller is the author of 10 books and more than 100 magazine articles, many of them on New England subjects. Since 1970 he has made his home in Vermont and Massachusetts, and has traveled and vacationed extensively in New Hampshire. Mr. Scheller is a former editor of *Appalachia,* the journal of the Appalachian Mountain Club, an organization that maintains its field headquarters and a chain of back-country huts in the White Mountains.

# Contents

Introduction    6

CHAPTER ONE
How New Hampshire
Came to Be    14

New Hampshire Map    16

CHAPTER TWO
The Seacoast    32

CHAPTER THREE
The Merrimack Valley    44

CHAPTER FOUR
The Connecticut Valley    56

CHAPTER FIVE
Central New Hampshire
& The Lakes Region    70

CHAPTER SIX
The White Mountains    80

CHAPTER SEVEN
The North Country    96

For Further Reading    103

*Photographs—front cover, left:* At North Conway. JEFF GNASS
*Right:* Ashuelot River. JAMES RANDKLEV; *back cover:* Mt. Jefferson and
the White Mountains from U.S. Route 3. CLYDE H. SMITH
*Title page:* Birch and maple leaves on moss, White Mountains.
GEORGE WUERTHNER
*Page 2, left:* Raindrop on an aspen leaf. TED LEVIN; *right:* Waterfall
through granite in Franconia Notch State Park. TOM TILL
*Page 3:* In Grafton County. TOM BEAN
*Facing page:* Portsmouth Harbor. CLYDE H. SMITH
*Left top:* The Madison Spring Hut on Mt. Adams. NONA BAUER
*Left:* Near North Conway. CLYDE H. SMITH

# Introduction

*Milkweed pods break open to release their seeds on the edge of a New Hampshire meadow.*
TED LEVIN

**Right:** *A fishing boat is surrounded by an armada of pleasure craft at Rye Harbor on the New Hampshire seacoast.* GEORGE WUERTHNER

**Facing page:** *Arethusa Falls, New Hampshire's highest, spills down a mountainside in Crawford Notch State Park.* GEORGE WUERTHNER

It is perhaps the oddest motto any state has ever put on an automobile license plate. Elsewhere in the Republic, bumper-mounted boosterism is limited to innocuous lines such as "Land of 10.000 Lakes," or "Land of Lincoln." New Jersey is the "Garden State," while West Virginia borrows from the John Denver song and pronounces itself "Almost Heaven." But New Hampshire will have nothing of such cheery blather. Pull up behind a New Hampshire car, and you will not be enticed to spend a vacation in the White Mountains or subjected to boasts about agricultural production. You will instead meet eye to eye with the official state philosophy: "Live Free or Die."

The phrase was coined by General John Stark, a thorny old character who fought the British at Bunker Hill and beat them at Bennington. There can't be any doubt about what Stark meant by his admonition, since he followed it himself quite literally. (He lived free, and died 40 years after the Revolution ended.) But what does the General's quote mean in the context of acres of automobiles parked at the Fox Run Mall in Portsmouth or outside a factory in Nashua, or on a pickup truck rolling down Route 16 through the Androscoggin Valley?

It's anyone's guess. A Boston liberal might tell you that the plates, first minted over a decade ago, represent a chip on New Hampshire's shoulder, a rallying cry of the "Better Dead than Red" variety left over from the superpatriot 1950s. A New Hampshire conservative might agree, archly adding that if invasion comes it will likely be from the People's Republic of Massachusetts. But the real reason behind such a flinty and uncompromising bit of license-plate propaganda most likely goes beyond politics, and lies deep within New Hampshire's ancient self-image. It is intended to summon the memory of archetypal New Hampshiremen like Stark himself, who told his men at the Battle of Bennington that the enemy would be theirs or "Molly Stark is a widow tonight"; or of Daniel Webster, who frequently, though probably erroneously, is credited with saying of the Franconia Notch rock formation called the Old Man of the Mountains that "in the mountains of New Hampshire God Almighty has hung out a sign to

*Autumn colors stand out against the stark white walls of a village church. This Episcopal Church, in North Conway, is something of an architectural anomaly, built in the board-and-batten carpenter gothic style of the mid-19th century rather than along the traditional lines inspired by Palladio and Christopher Wren.*
JEFF GNASS

show that there he makes men." And God makes them, so New Hampshire people like to think, out of granite.

To a substantial degree, New Hampshire's notion of itself has drifted into the consciousness of the rest of the nation. Like Maine and Vermont, New Hampshire is often seen as the New Englander's New England, a sort of regional quin-

tessence: here are the white-steepled churches, the covered bridges, the self-reliant yeomen farmers celebrated in the poems and very character of that craggy and crusty sometime New Hampshireman, Robert Frost. Never mind that the old Yankee stock has long since been tempered by waves of foreign immigration, or that for more than a hundred years New Hampshire's economy has been more industrial than agricultural, its population more urban than rural. This is the New Hampshire people want, and this is the New Hampshire they will have.

Another powerful contributor towards the building of New Hampshire's national image comes quadrennially, in the form of the state's presidential primary. Media coverage of the Republican and Democratic primaries often is the only opportunity people outside New England have to focus on New Hampshire in what television newspeople call "real time," as opposed to the realms of history or myth. What they learn often puts a quirky edge on the yeoman farmer stereotype. They may see a front-runner cut down to size, or (as with Lyndon Johnson in 1968) a sitting president humbled at the polls. They will surely hear more direct questions posed to the candidates, since campaigning in a state this size is more a matter of personal appearances at the town hall or in voters' living rooms than the packaged "media events" that characterize the bigger markets. Throughout the season that culminates in the February vote, Americans far from the banks of the Connecticut or the Merrimack will be privy to the shrill pronunciamentos of Manchester's mercurial *Union Leader,* the arch-reactionary newspaper built by the late William Loeb and used by him to place a powerful stamp on New Hampshire's political agenda. To the *Union Leader,* it's all a matter of which Republican is the least traitorous, and which Democrat the most. And the distant primary observer may even learn something of New Hampshire's intramural politics, such as the tacit requirement that gubernatorial candidates "take the pledge" against ever supporting the imposition of state income or sales taxes. Any politician who proposes that New Hampshire citizens should no longer live free in this regard will surely die at the polls. All in all, a spectator's seat at New Hampshire primary time—whether in Massachusetts or New Mexico—is likely to be an education in just how cantankerously independent the descendants of Frost's yeomen can be.

It could be that New Hampshire has never gotten the frontier spirit out of its system. Of course, this little province in the longest-settled

corner of the United States is hardly a "frontier" in the 19th-century Western or modern Alaskan sense of the term, but the time was when it was quite literally New England's frontier, the place where coast-dwellers went when they felt the need for breathing room and cheap, uncultivated land. There's a good reason why so many upper Connecticut Valley towns on both the Vermont

*A bright fall day in Littleton. The white, columned structure on the right side of the street is Thayers Inn, a Main Street institution since 1843.* CHRISTIAN HEEB

and New Hampshire sides of the river bear the names of communities in Massachusetts, and why the Granite State has a "New Ipswich" named after the old one in the Bay State. Before restless souls could head very far west, they headed north. If we head far enough north in their footsteps, we find that to this day the names of individual pioneers remain attached to sparsely-settled townships in the White Mountains and beyond—places like Pinkham's Grant, Martin's Location, and Thompson and Meserve's Purchase.

Two of the most famous of all the New Hampshire pioneers lent their name to one of the great passes, or "notches," that runs north and south through the White Mountains. Abel Crawford came to the mountains as a trapper in the early 1790s, and for many years he and his son Ethan Allen Crawford ran the only inn for travelers making their difficult way through Crawford Notch. Ethan Allen Crawford's heroic feats of climbing and trailblazing still are legend in New Hampshire. It was he, the story goes, who stood on the summit of Mt. Washington with seven of his friends, one day in 1820, and named the peaks of the Presidential Range with mighty cheers and toasts of rum. Massachusetts, so near and yet so far, has no heroes like Abel and Ethan Allen Crawford. In the Bay Colony's earliest days, anyone half so exuberant would have been censured by the Puritan divines. Easterners though they may have remained, the Crawfords belonged more to the world of Davy Crockett and Daniel Boone. If they couldn't have lived free, they gladly would have died.

But like every other place in an era when people move from state to state more quickly than they once would have moved around the corner, New Hampshire in the late 1980s stands only partly on tradition. There are people of different traditions—French Canadians in Manchester or Berlin, for whom New Hampshire began the day *Grandpère* arrived from Trois-Rivières to work in the mill—and also those of no local tradition at all. What do Stark, Webster and Crawford have to do with someone who arrived in southern New Hampshire last year, to buy a condominium in Nashua and work in high technology? In many

cases, people come to New Hampshire to put down what passes for roots nowadays because there are income and sales taxes on the other side of the border, in Massachusetts. This is hardly the most profound or lofty-spirited declaration of independence a person can make (neither is the decision of the developer who chooses to build in New Hampshire rather than Vermont because of the latter state's more stringent environmental laws), but the fact is that motives have a way of looking more heroic than practical when perceived across a gap of centuries. It's a safe bet that

many if not most of those Granite State pioneers journeyed up the river valleys and through the notches simply because they wanted a little less of Boston in their lives. There's a bumper sticker making the rounds lately that reads "Live Free or Live in Massachusetts," and if it had been available to put on horsecarts in 1790 it might have been a common sight indeed.

For all our attempts to define the character of New Hampshire through its people, we can come to only a partial understanding of the place if we

**Above:** *Browsing at an antique shop in Conway. Like the rest of New England, New Hampshire does a brisk business in treasures from its past.* BRUCE BERG
**Left:** *One of the graceful Georgian doorways of Portsmouth. This one led to new Hampshire's first printing shop.* GEORGE WUERTHNER

**Facing page:** *The summit of Mount Washington, highest point in the northeastern United States. Snow in October is commonplace on the 6,288' peak.* TOM TILL

*Above:* *"Build thee more stately mansions": along the New Hampshire coast near Rye Beach, turn-of-the-century industrialists and merchant princes took the biblical line at face value. In our own Roaring Eighties, a few grand houses still are being built along this prime oceanfront strip.* GEORGE WUERTHNER

*Right top:* *What happened to November? The only indication here of a season between Halloween and Christmas is the camouflage hunting hat.* CHRISTIAN HEEB

*Right bottom:* *Live free or die: a mailbox near Berlin.* CHRISTIAN HEEB

fail to consider the terrain. There is in fact a succession of terrains here; if we were to work our way north from the scant 16 miles of seacoast to the headwaters of the Connecticut at the Canadian border, we might be tempted to define the landscape as prelude followed by climax followed by anticlimax. Beyond Portsmouth harbor there extends a great bay (appropriately called The Great Bay) surrounded by salt marsh, but to the north and west the land soon becomes hilly and forested in mixed hardwoods. The valley of the Merrimack splits the southern part of the state into eastern and western halves; west of the cities whose mill wheels the Merrimack once turned the land rises again, dropping off beyond Mt. Monadnock and the southern hill towns to the fertile dairylands along the broad Connecticut. Throughout this part of New Hampshire, the landscape could be that of Massachusetts, or of Vermont on either side of its Green Mountain spine.

New Hampshire has no such longitudinal spine of mountains. As Robert Frost once wrote, "The Vermont mountains stretch extended straight/ New Hampshire mountains curl up in a coil." It is that coiled, secluded aspect of the White Mountains that makes such a mysterious fastness of them. Strike high ground north of Concord and there they loom, distant and somber, beyond the skein of blue lakes that pock the center of the state. North of Lake Winnipesaukee rise the southern sentinels of the Whites, Chocorua and Passaconaway; from here on, the coil grows tighter and the peaks higher. At the center is the range-within-a-range called the Presidentials, with 6,288′ Mt. Washington standing as the pinnacle not only of New England but of all the northeastern United States. There are only three passes through Frost's coil of mountains, and their names are far more famous than the numbers of the modern roads that follow them: Pinkham Notch, Crawford Notch, Franconia Notch.

Beyond Mt. Madison, the northern outpost of the Presidentials, the mountains suddenly uncoil and stand peppered across Coös County as isolated peaks. The northern tip of New Hampshire is a vast conifer forest, almost a wilderness still. Follow Route 16 along the rushing Androscoggin River and you may as well be in the farthest reaches of Maine; take Route 3 past Colebrook and Pittsburg and you will reach the three big lakes, at the very top of New Hampshire, that spill into the Connecticut River, brooklike as it starts its way to Long Island Sound. There are hardly any people up here—far fewer, oddly enough, than there are north of the nearby border where the Québecois have cut the forest and made farms. New Hampshire begins with a press of population at the Massachusetts border and the sea; it ends at the Third Connecticut Lake with no one home.

---

This book is about the land that lies between those two geographic extremes, and the people who make it their home. It is about living, free or not as any of us are, within that difficult and magnificent terrain.

*Looking more than passably fit after a century of service, a covered bridge spans the fledgling Pemigewasset in Franconia Notch.* TOM TILL

# CHAPTER ONE

# How New Hampshire Came To Be

***Above:*** *Portsmouth believes in fresh paint—at least it has since the revival of the 1960s and 1970s.* TOM BEAN

***Right:*** *Looking southwest from the Sandwich Range, White Mountain National Forest. In the 19th century, virtually all of this territory was cut over for timber or agriculture.* GEORGE WUERTHNER

***Facing page:*** *The summit of Mt. Monadnock, scoured clean the way the glaciers left it.* STEPHEN TRIMBLE

With the world so old and humanity such a recent arrival, New Hampshire like every other inhabited place must be said to have two histories. The first is the story of events in what John McPhee has called "deep time," the eons required to shape the earth as mankind found it. The second, occupying only a tiny sliver of time, concerns the making of human society in New Hampshire.

## Prehistory: Geology and Natural Setting

If any state ever had a sobriquet suggestive of solidness and immutability, surely it is the Granite State. And if there is a physical distillation of that sense of pride in permanence, it is the Old Man of the Mountains in Franconia Notch. Yet the Old Man is only yesterday's construction, a creature of the last Ice Age, and there was a time when granite itself was freshly introduced into the landscape of New Hampshire. If we can manage to compress deep time to understandable dimensions, and sidestep our inability to actually comprehend the concept of hundreds of millions of years, it is possible to arrive at a picture of how New Hampshire was formed.

The substratum of New Hampshire, the basement of rock upon which the modern surface of the state has been laid, is essentially a complex structure of metamorphic gneiss and schist with a grain running roughly northwest to southeast. Beginning in the late Devonian period, some 350 million years ago, the tortuously folded schists and gneisses of the region were subjected to successive intrusions of molten material, primarily granite and syenite. Cooled and solidified masses of granite, known as batholiths where they are exposed at the surface, are apparent today at Concord and Milford and in belts east of Lake Winnipesaukee, west through the White Mountains from Conway and along the Connecticut Valley. Exposed intrusions of syenite and similar rock occur along a northwest-southeast axis from the northern tip of New Hampshire almost to its seacoast, and account for such mountain formations as Tripyramid, in Waterville, and the Belknap Range south of Lake Winnipesaukee.

By the end of the Permian Age, approximately 225 million years ago, the metamorphic schists and gneisses of New Hampshire and the igneous intrusions to which they had been subjected were heavily layered with an accumulation of sedimentary sand, clay and gravel. There followed the upheavals of the Alleghenian Event at the close of the Paleozoic Era, of which the Permian Age was the final period; this raised the hardened sediment and its understructure into

high mountains that were in turn leveled by the erosion processes of the Mesozoic Era. By the close of the Mesozoic, about 65 million years ago, most of New Hampshire was a near-level plain punctuated by mountains of erosion-resistant material.

The next step in the sculpting of the Granite State was a combination of the raising of the plain, by means of an upwarping early in the Tertiary Period some 50 to 60 million years ago and its continued erosion by valley-cutting streams. The stage was now set for a far more recent event, the Ice Ages of the Pleistocene Epoch. There were at least four separate cycles of glacial advance and retreat in the Pleistocene, lasting from about 1 million to 12,000 years ago. The masses of ice scraped and scoured the surface of New Hamp-

shire, leaving erratic boulders at the very top of Mt. Washington and gouging the floors of the state's hundreds of lakes and ponds. The drumlin hills that lie between the Connecticut and Merrimack valleys were created as compacted glacial till was left behind by the retreating ice. The valleys and notches of mountain regions were channeled from their original V-shapes into more rounded proportions. Vast inland areas were inundated as meltwater lay in depressed basins of earth and icebound debris choked drainage to the sea. Finally, the unplugging of these glacial dams combined with the process called "isostatic rebound"—the uplifting of land relieved of the glaciers' pressure—to create the present-day configuration of lakeshores and riverbanks. Nothing on earth is ever completed, but by the end of the last

Ice Age nature had finished building the only New Hampshire that human beings ever have known.

People have, however, seen New Hampshire clothed differently. From the time vegetation first took hold after the glacier, until the beginning of English settlement more than 350 years ago, forests spread to cover all but a tiny fraction of the state's 6 million acres. The prevalence of particular species depended upon soil and climate, and upon the extent to which fire created openings for early and later successional shrubs, preludes to the return of climax forest. Hardwoods generally held sway throughout the south, although this kingdom of the birches, maples, beeches and oaks was hardly devoid of coniferous trees: right through the 18th century, the Piscataqua Valley yielded lordly white pines to serve as the masts of sailing vessels. "Mast trees," they were called, and

in 1734 illegal harvesting of pines earmarked for the King's navy led to a "Mast Tree Riot" in Fremont when the royal government's surveyor general attempted to inspect the fallen timber.

Among the evergreens of the north, white pine came to dominate the hillsides south of the White Mountains, and spruce the north. Mixed among them are hemlock, balsam and some cedar. At the highest elevations of the Presidential Range, forestation gives way entirely, and alpine flora usually associated with far more northerly latitudes comes into its own.

This, as Longfellow wrote in *Evangeline,* is the forest primeval. Or rather it was. By the mid-1800s, only half of New Hampshire was forested. The demands of agriculture, construction, shipbuilding and the hungry new steam locomotives had led the settlers and their descendants to clear

3 million acres—an average of more than 13,600 acres a year over 220 years, not bad for people innocent of chain saws. But the forest has done an even better job of reclamation, now that agriculture has declined for more than a century and no wooden ships slide down the ways at Portsmouth. Today, about 86 percent of New Hampshire is covered with trees.

The birds and animals of New Hampshire are those of the northeastern woodlands generally. Three and a half centuries of white settlement, farming, deforestation and development have, of course, affected indigenous species with varying results. The white-tailed deer, an animal thriving upon the browse available as cleared land reverts to second growth, exists in greater numbers today than before the forests were cut. Bears nearly were extirpated from all but the far north 80 or 90 years ago, but now they are so well distributed throughout the state that one recently wandered into the northern Massachusetts city of Lawrence. (The moose, another species on the rebound in New Hampshire, also is known to make an occasional urban foray.) The wolf is long gone, but the fox has adapted and so has the bobcat. The mystery animal of New England is the mountain lion, known locally as the panther. Standard intelligence has it that the great cats have been extinct here for a century or more, but enough sober countrymen report sightings each year to convince some wildlife biologists that as many as 25 panthers survive between Massachusetts and Maine. If so, a few are doubtless in New Hampshire.

Several species of smaller creatures rise and fall in population in direct, rather than inverse, proportion to the presence of man. The porcupine and raccoon haunt the fringes of human settlement even in the suburbs, and find a special attraction in carelessly discarded garbage. And where there are porcupines there are their predators the fishers, large cousins of the minks and weasels, which once were hunted to the brink of extirpation because of their supposed destruction of game birds. There are also the creatures everyone wishes well: still-scarce heralds of environmental amelioration such as the Atlantic salmon, the bald eagle and the common loon.

## Indians and Possible Pre-Columbian Settlers

All of the native Americans living in what is now New Hampshire belonged to the Algonquian language group. There were two major confederations of New Hampshire Indians at the time the English settlers first arrived: the Abnaki, centered in the eastern part of the area near the present Maine border; and the Penacooks, living in central and southern New Hampshire along the valleys of the Pemigewasset and Merrimack Rivers. Each confederacy was made up of smaller tribes. The

*Above:* Far more at home on the fringes of farms than it ever was in the forest primeval, the white-tailed deer is abundant in New Hampshire. TED LEVIN

*Left:* For years, the fisher was unfairly accused of predation on game animals; now it is valued as a check on porcupine populations, and it is making a comeback in northern New England. This eleven-week-old dens with his mother and the rest of her litter in a hollowed red maple. TED LEVIN

*Facing page:* A young moose, its antlers in velvet, browses in a New Hampshire pond. CLYDE H. SMITH

*Above: If there was a settlement of Celts in New Hampshire long before the English landed, was this one of their sacrificial altars? The carefully-grooved tablet and surrounding stone structures, never satisfactorily explained, are at "America's Stonehenge," Mystery Hill, Salem, New Hampshire.* C. McGEE-MILLEY

*Facing page, left: The Penacook chief Passaconaway was revered by his people as a bearer of magical powers; when he died at 100 years of age, it was said he was borne into heaven on a sled drawn by wolves. But his magic could not bring about his fondest wish: peace between the Indians and whites.* COURTESY NEW HAMPSHIRE HISTORICAL SOCIETY

*Right: The Silver Cascade knifes through a fissure in a granite outcropping, Crawford Notch.* JAMES RANDKLEV

Abnaki (closely related to the Micmac of Canada) incorporated the Anasgunticook of the Androscoggin Valley; the Pequawkets at the headwaters of the Saco River; and the Sokoki, who hunted along the Saco and planted crops near its mouth at Saco Bay in Maine. Among the Penacook tribes were the Amoskeags near what is now Manchester; the Nashuas along the river to which they gave their name; the Piscataquas at Portsmouth; the Squamscots near Exeter; and the Pemigewassets and Winnipesaukees of the central lakes region. Along the eastern shore of Lake Winnipesaukee near Paugus Bay was a seasonal encampment of the Penacooks called Aquadochtan, said to have been one of the largest Indian villages in New England. Present-day Weirs Beach, at Lake

Winnipesaukee near the now-enlarged channel leading into Paugus Bay, takes its name from the tremendously productive fishing weirs that the Indians built and tended here year after year. (The Winnipesaukee area is also thought to have been inhabited by an even earlier native culture, a pre-Algonquian group called the "Red Paint People.") Numbering perhaps no more than 4,000 at the time the English arrived, the Abnakis and Penacooks led a semi-nomadic existence organized around seasonal cycles of hunting and fishing, and a rudimentary agriculture based upon corn, beans, squashes and tobacco.

It isn't certain that the first Indian contact with white men in what was to be New Hampshire occurred when the English arrived in the early 17th century. There is general agreement that Basque and Portuguese fishermen were using sites along the New England coast for setting up fish-drying flakes during the century preceding its purported "discovery"; and nowadays the idea that Norsemen visited the region circa 1000 A.D. no longer is considered radically revisionist by academic historians. But even the Vikings appear to have been latecomers, if we accept certain theories put forward to explain the stone chambers and related structures at a place called Mystery Hill in North Salem. Like similar low stone buildings at sites throughout New England, these were assumed by the first English settlers to have been built by long-gone Indians. The colonists' own descendants took them to be their forefathers' root cellars (many were partially if not completely subterranean), and either used them as such or tore them apart to make stone walls. Only in our century has anyone seriously suspected they may have an entirely different and more distant origin.

In his 1976 book *America B.C.*, Barry Fell drew a remarkable set of conclusions regarding Mystery Hill. First, he pointed out, the construction of these "root cellars" closely resembled that of similar buildings erected by Bronze Age Celts in Europe. Second, several of the standing henge stones at the North Salem site are positioned in alignment with the setting sun on the days of the summer and winter solstices and equinox. Finally, Fell claimed that he and others combing the struc-

tures at Mystery Hill found stones inscribed with pre-Christian Iberian Punic and Celtic Ogam characters indicating the dedication of a temple to the Phoenician god Baal. It was clear, wrote Fell, "that ancient Celts had built the New England megalithic chambers and that Phoenician mariners were welcome visitors." The inscriptions appear to have been made between 800 and 600 B.C.; radiocarbon dating shows that the site could have been occupied as early as the second millennium B.C.

What the ancestors of the Penacooks and Abnakis may have thought of all this hasn't been recorded. Even more fascinating is the question of whether the Indians modern settlers encountered may have been part Celtic, at least in their language. Certain similarities in vocabulary are almost too coincidental. While the academic community considers what to believe, we can all go examine the evidence for ourselves. The stone structures at Mystery Hill are managed as an archaeological preserve and are open to visitors. The disappearance of New England's native population was the result of more than a century of gradual withdrawal to the north. The middle years of the 17th century were marked by relatively civil relations

between the colonists and Indians, but by the time of the general uprising of eastern New England Indians known as King Philip's War (1675), the pressures of advancing colonization and the bitterness of broken promises had led even the normally peaceful Penacooks to disregard the dying wish of their great chief Passaconaway for peace with the white man. Passaconaway's son, Chief Wonalancet, led many of his people away to Canada, but Wonalancet's nephew Kancamagus led

others in an attack on Dover in 1689. The New Hampshire Indians, drawn further into alliances with the French, retreated toward Canada during the 1700s. They waged an off-and-on guerrilla campaign against the frontier settlements, burning villages and taking captives back to Quebec. The last Indian raid in New Hampshire was in the Androscoggin Valley, on the eve of the American Revolution in 1774.

*Above:* Yellow birches on Peabody Creek in the Mahoosuc Mountains.

*Facing page:* Sunset over Silver Lake, in the central lakes region of New Hampshire. GEORGE WUERTHNER PHOTOS

## First Explorations and English Settlements

The first modern Europeans acknowledged to have visited the coast of New Hampshire made no attempt to stay. In June of 1603, Captain Martin Pring piloted his two British vessels *Speedwell* and *Discoverer* into the mouth of the Piscataqua. He had come looking not for land or for gold but for beaver pelts and the medicinal herb sassafras. Walking the river bank where the city of Portsmouth now stands, he found no sassafras—nor did he meet any Indians with which to trade his trinkets for furs. Pring soon weighed anchor and left for home, by way of Plymouth Bay in Massachusetts.

For a few days two summers later, the French flag flew over Piscataqua Bay, as the ubiquitous Samuel de Champlain nosed into the harbor before making his landfall down the coast near Rye. For nine years no more visitors came, until in 1614 that other peripatetic explorer, Captain John Smith, touched upon the Isles of Shoals 10 miles out from the banks of the Piscataqua during the course of a voyage from the mouth of Maine's Penobscot River down to Cape Cod. True to form, he named the isles after himself and continued on his way.

Having mapped the New England coast and written a book to promote its settlement, Smith in 1620 became instrumental in securing a royal charter for the Council for New England, which was empowered to distribute grants of land between the Hudson and the St. Lawrence. One of the larger of those grants was made to Captain John Mason and Sir Fernando Gorges, who were given patent to the lands between the Merrimack and Kennebec rivers. In 1629, the partners split their domain, with Mason taking claim to that portion of the coast that lay between the mouths of the Piscataqua and the Merrimack, and inland for 60 miles. The scope of New Hampshire's short seacoast was now roughly set. The province's name was likewise soon settled upon by Mason, whose native English county had been Hampshire.

Meanwhile, a Council for New England clerk named David Thomson had received a small land grant within the boundaries of Mason's patent. Thomson in 1623 led a party of emigrants to found a fishing and trading center at Odiorne's Point, just south of modern Portsmouth, that today is considered to be the first of New Hampshire's English settlements. Another, at Hilton's Point (now Dover), followed in 1631. In that same year a charter was given to planters from Massachusetts for a township called Piscataqua, the ancestor of Portsmouth. By 1640 the towns at Piscataqua Odiorne's Point and Dover had been joined by settlements at Hampton and Exeter, the latter founded by Rev. John Wheelwright and a band of fellow religious dissidents from Massachusetts. One thousand English colonists lived in these communities planted within Mason's grant, to no advantage of Captain Mason himself. He had died in 1635, financially drained by underwriting his New Hampshire ventures. The towns in his domain, once to have been the cornerstones of his feudal prosperity, struggled along with no real interference from his heirs or any proper notion of their political status. (The Council for New England expired the same year as Mason.) Mason's principal legacy was an incredible tangle of land-

claim litigation that occupied his heirs, off and on, until 1787. New Hampshire was not to be a tidily organized fiefdom managed by a rich man in London.

## New Hampshire in the Colonial Period

If John Mason wasn't to control the fledgling communities of New Hampshire, neither were they long to control themselves. By 1641, the four towns of Portsmouth, Dover, Exeter and Hampton had to admit that they had been unsuccessful in forming a mutual government, and that they were unable to stand alone as what amounted to tiny

sovereign republics. The citizens thus applied to Massachusetts to be put under the larger colony's jurisdiction. The pact that ensued made the New Hampshire towns a part of the Massachusetts Bay Colony for the next 38 years. Although subject to the criminal and civil laws of Massachusetts, the little coastal enclaves north of the Merrimack retained, in practice, a good deal of regional autonomy. Town meetings elected officers, established local ordinances and decided issues pertaining to education. Most important, they were not bound by Massachusetts' stringent regulations regarding Congregational (Puritan) church membership as a

*Village church, Shelburne. The religion the early settlers brought to inland towns generally was of a dissenting strain that ran counter to the Anglicanism of Portsmouth.* CLYDE H. SMITH

the interior, New Hampshire resolutely faced the sea. With the exception of Exeter, all of the towns between the Merrimack and the Piscataqua were directly on the coast or Great Bay; and even Exeter had access to the bay via the Squamscott River. In their insularity and preoccupation with trade—fish, lumber and furs were the principal commodities—the New Hampshire settlements resembled the French Canadian outposts along the St. Lawrence more than their immediate neighbors to the south. And as the 17th century drew to a close, Indian raids instigated in part by the French served as a powerful deterrent to colonization far from the garrisons of the coast.

In 1679, New Hampshire began another experiment as a political entity independent of Massachusetts. King Charles II declared the colony a separate royal province, and appointed a succession of royal governors to rule in conjunction with a governor's council (also chosen by the king) and a popularly elected assembly. This move on the part of the British government was inspired less by a desire to grant New Hampshire a measure of autonomy than by a hope to trim Massachusetts' sails. Already the Bay Colony was growing fractious under the more centralized controls imposed by the crown after the restoration of the British monarchy; from 1686 to the "Glorious Revolution" of 1688, this restiveness came to a head as New England chafed under the rule of the hated governor Sir Edmund Andros. The satraps sent to preside over New Hampshire were equally disliked, so much so that in 1698 the smaller colony once again sought union with Massachusetts. From that year until 1741, the two provinces shared the same governor, although they kept their own legislatures and governor's councils. This is not to say that all was in harmony among the communities on either side of the Merrimack. While not fighting the French and Indians to the north, New Hampshiremen spent much of the early 1700s engaged in boundary disputes with the authorities in Boston. The affected areas lay not only along the Massachusetts-New Hampshire border, but to the north and east as well: until it became a state in 1820, Maine was part of Massachusetts. It wasn't until 1740 that King George II decided the case to

prerequisite for voting and holding political office. The four towns were required to send representatives to the General Court, or colonial legislature, in Boston; but it was not stipulated that the New Hampshire delegates be church members. Still, Puritan Congregationalism remained the official church of Hampton, Dover and Exeter. Only Portsmouth, regal as ever in its predilections, officially adopted the Anglican faith.

Throughout the years in which they were part of Massachusetts, the original townships of New Hampshire expanded very little outside their original precincts. No significant inland settlement was made until the founding of Nashua, in 1673. Whereas Massachusetts proper began to balance its fishing, shipbuilding and seafaring concerns with the development of farming communities in

the great advantage of New Hampshire and finally fixed the colony's southern and eastern borders in their present form. (The question of the western border, with Vermont, would amount to another fine mess in the years just after the American Revolution.) A year later, in 1741, King George appointed a separate governor for New Hampshire. The two domains would never again be one, either as colony or state.

Although the governors of Massachusetts-New Hampshire kept their residence and headquarters in Boston prior to the final split in 1741, the real seat of authority in the northern province was at Portsmouth, where New Hampshire's lieutenant governor presided. In 1717, the first truly effective authority in the colony appeared in the person of Lieutenant-Governor John Wentworth, grandson of one of the original settlers of Exeter and first in what was virtually a dynastic line of Wentworths that governed New Hampshire until the beginning of the American Revolution. A wealthy merchant who typified the growing power and sophistication of Portsmouth, John Wentworth proved to be a practical and effective administrator whose accomplishments included a peace treaty with the Indians (1725), a general advancement in commerce and the encouragement of settlements far inland from New Hampshire's traditional coastal enclaves. By 1732, two years after Lieutenant-Governor Wentworth died in office, the colony's population of 12,000 was distributed not only among the four original towns but among far-flung communities such as Londonderry, Rochester and the future state capital of Concord (first known as Penacook).

The greatest of New Hampshire's colonial administrators was John Wentworth's son, Benning Wentworth. Appointed governor at the time King George II formally separated New Hampshire from Massachusetts in 1741, the younger Wentworth presided for 25 years over an unprecedented period of growth and prosperity. During his term of office, 124 new townships were granted, including many carved out of territory that would have been considered forbidding wilderness just a few decades earlier; by the time of his retirement in 1766, New Hampshire's citizens

**Above:** *Birches near Shelburne. The white birch is New Hampshire's protean hardwood: it provided the tough skin of the Indians' canoes, and the bending yet enduring central image of one of Robert Frost's most famous poems.*
**Left:** *Seabrook harbor, surrounded by salt marshes and protected from the open Atlantic. Of the towns along New Hampshire's short coastline, only Portsmouth had a natural harbor expansive enough to support large-scale shipbuilding and a sizeable commercial fleet.*
GEORGE WUERTHNER PHOTOS

numbered 52,000. Portsmouth became a city of gracious Georgian mansions—none so great as that of Governor Wentworth himself—and handsome churches, of bustling wharves and counting-houses. Where wary pioneers had not long before kept guard at barricaded doors, periwigged magnificoes drew crystal decanters of imported Madeira from mahogany sideboards. Governor Wentworth set this style, but his lavish and expansive manner was balanced by real ability at juggling the interests of the crown, of the British entrepreneurs who profited from New England exports and of his own enterprising and energetic fellow colonists. Through an elaborate patronage system, he managed to exercise almost complete control

of the courts, the governor's council and even the assembly. But the governor was no despot who bled his domain for his own advantage; for the most part, the colony prospered along with him.

In one particular regard, though, Benning Wentworth's penchant for self-enrichment went a bit too far. In making his township grants in the unsettled parts of the New Hampshire interior, the governor always reserved from 500 to 800 acres of each newly chartered town for himself. By this means he eventually acquired 100,000 acres of some of the choicest land in the colony, much of it destined to skyrocket in value as settlement and development advanced. As long as he managed to keep up his London connections, maintain tight

control of the province from Portsmouth, and report good profits on timber cutting and shipbuilding, no one objected to his hand in the till. But when these three elements of his power began to weaken, Wentworth's enemies called him to task for his land schemes and nearly forced his dismissal. His nephew, John Wentworth, convinced the authorities to allow the durable old governor to resign—and in the following year, 1767, he secured the appointment for himself.

John Wentworth was the last of the Wentworth dynasty and the last colonial governor of New Hampshire. An exceptionally able and conscientious man, he was the first of the colony's administrators to recognize the concerns of the rapidly growing inland settlements, which he attempted to link with the seacoast by means of a new system of roads. One of the third Governor Wentworth's most ambitious road-building projects was the hewing of a route through the back country from Portsmouth to newly-chartered Dartmouth College, on the Connecticut River in Hanover, by way of his own summer estate in Wolfeborough on Lake Winnipesaukee. (The idea that the governor would hold court this far from the seacoast haven of Portsmouth gives some idea of how civilized New Hampshire south of the White Mountains had become during its first 150 years.) Well liked and prudent enough to avoid the avaricious excesses of his uncle in matters of township chartering, John Wentworth may have lasted as governor well into the 19th century—if it hadn't been for the American Revolution.

Separatist sentiment in New Hampshire surfaced primarily among the very segment of colonial society that Governor Wentworth had been trying to bring into the mainstream: the outpost settlements in the central and western part of the province. The yeomen of the New Hampshire hill towns were Congregationalist farmers and tradesmen, as opposed to the Anglican merchants of Portsmouth; even if American independence had not loomed as an issue, enmity between the two classes was bound to develop. (Just such an urban-rural economic split was behind Shays' Rebellion in the newly-independent Massachusetts of the 1780s, while a strong sense of regional separatism led Vermonters to sever their ties with New Hampshire before the war was even over.) British attempts at repression in the colonies during the early 1770s simply brought these feelings to a head, so much so that even the citizens of Portsmouth, in 1773, held a public meeting at which they adopted 11 resolutions on American rights and liberties. By the watershed year of 1776, it is estimated that only seven percent of New Hampshire's adult white male population opposed the American position in the war effort (the figure is based upon responses to the Continental Congress's "Association Test," in which men were asked whether or not they would commit themselves to armed resistance.)

What happened in New Hampshire in 1776 was no longer any concern of John Wentworth's. By December of 1774, the situation in his province had deteriorated to the point where he could not even effect the arrest of 400 patriots who had removed the gunpowder from Fort William and Mary, in Portsmouth, while detaining the fort's commander and his British troops. On August 24 of the following year, Governor Wentworth left his capital never to return. He later became governor of another British colony, Nova Scotia, and held this position for many years.

*Above:* The Old Parsonage, Newington, built in 1710. *A handsomely restored specimen of early 18th century New Hampshire architecture, and a textbook example of the saltbox style.* GEORGE WUERTHNER
*Facing page, left: John Wentworth, first of an illustrious line of New Hampshire administrators. He was lieutenant-governor in charge of the province, 1717-1730. Center: Benning Wentworth, greatest of the line. An able steward of the province for a quarter century, he grew rich by skimming choice acreage as he chartered new towns. Right: The third Wentworth, also named John, was Britain's final governor of New Hampshire.* IMAGES COURTESY NEW HAMPSHIRE HISTORICAL SOCIETY

*Pioneer settlers of the Connecticut Valley rest in a churchyard at Lyme.* TOM BEAN

## The Revolutionary and Federal Periods

The colonial era in New Hampshire was over. Men of the First, Second and Third New Hampshire Regiments fought from Bunker Hill to Yorktown (the First served continuously for eight and a half years), and more than a hundred lightly-armed privateers sailed from Portsmouth to wage the maritime equivalent of guerrilla war on British shipping. For all its participation in the war, however, New Hampshire was spared from participation in direct hostilities. It was the only state of the original 13 never invaded by British forces.

New Hampshire was also the first of the former colonies to declare its independence from the Crown. This was the de facto result of the Provincial Congress's adopting, early in January of 1776, a temporary constitution vesting authority in a bicameral legislature. This document, which went into effect six months before the signing of the Declaration of Independence, continued to regulate New Hampshire's affairs until the state constitution was adopted in 1784.

Delegates from the 175 towns of New Hampshire had another constitution to consider during the spring of 1788. This was, of course, the federal document drafted in Philadelphia the previous summer and already ratified by six states. Two other states voted for ratification during a two-month adjournment of the New Hampshire convention, so that when the delegates reconvened on June 18 they had the opportunity of casting the ninth and deciding vote towards adoption of the Constitution. They took that step three days later, 57 to 46, and the Federal Era began.

Like the rest of coastal New England, New Hampshire's seaport communities stood to benefit mightily from the new freedom in trade that American independence promised. And for all practical purposes, New Hampshire's great mercantile center was Portsmouth. The yards of Portsmouth, which had built fishing and trading vessels in colonial times and at least three warships during the Revolution, were set again to peacetime work, and the merchants of the town used the new ships to turn handsome profits. The *haute bourgeois* glory of the old Benning Wentworth days was revived, as Federal Portsmouth joined the Massachusetts towns of Boston, Salem and Newburyport in reaping the rewards of global trade. In 1823, Governor Levi Woodbury calculated that Portsmouth's exports had quadrupled over the preceding three decades, as had the gross value of the state's farm and forest products. As for population, the total of 52,000 at the arrival of the second Governor John Wentworth in 1766 had multiplied to nearly 184,000 by 1800 and to almost a quarter million 20 years later.

But despite the prominence and grandeur of Portsmouth, New Hampshire at the beginning of the 19th century was already outgrowing its old image of a sophisticated seaport capital attached to a straggling collection of isolated country towns. The road-building projects begun by governor John Wentworth prior to the Revolution continued after independence, so that communication between the Connecticut Valley and the sea was no longer so difficult as to make the valley towns virtual entities unto themselves (several had even cast their lot with Vermont, and intended to join the new Green Mountain State before the boundary was finally fixed at the Connecticut River in 1782). The New Hampshire Turnpike between Portsmouth and Concord was incorporated in 1796, and by 1808 the latter town had taken over from Portsmouth as state capital.

There were other signs that, south of the White Mountains, the boondocks weren't quite the boondocks any more. Dartmouth College, whose Latin motto translates as "A Voice Crying in the Wilderness," opened its medical school at Hanover in 1798. Phillips Academy at Exeter was founded in 1781, and 10 years later it was joined by academies in Atkinson and Amherst. Pursuits other than subsistence agriculture began to occupy the inland villages. The spinning of flax into linen long had been practiced by the Scotch-Irish settlers around Peterborough, and even before the Revolution their output was sufficient to make linen an item for export as well as local use. Perhaps the most famous of all the Federal era's "cottage industries" in New Hampshire was the cabinetmaking business carried on by three generations of the Dunlap family in south-central towns such as Chester, Bedford, Henniker and Goffstown. The name Dunlap is pure magic for today's dealers and aficionados of American furniture; it represents the last flowering of the 18th century tradition in an era when craftsmen were turning increasingly to the more severe Sheraton and Hepplewhite styles. Remarkably, nearly all of the Dunlaps' work was done in country towns of fewer than 2,000 people.

But the future of New Hampshire lay not in furniture, nor in any of the other hand crafts. It was written instead in water. In 1803, the Souhegan River at New Ipswich was harnessed by

*Above:* Early morning calm on the Merrimack River near Concord. It couldn't have looked much different to Henry David Thoreau in 1839.
*Left:* The textile industry, mighty engine of the New Hampshire economy for a century, had its beginnings in this New Ipswich mill. GEORGE WUERTHNER PHOTOS

Benjamin Prichard to power the state's first cotton mill. The venture lasted only a short time before Prichard turned his attention to a larger river, the Merrimack. In 1809, at the Amoskeag Falls where Manchester now stands, he built a new mill that would grow to become the largest textile factory in the world.

duction of what had been a locally- or even domestically-made item. Second, they opened up an avenue of employment other than farming and hand crafts. In New Hampshire and New England generally, the textile mills and shoe factories drew their workers directly from the farms. Young rural women were preferred as "operatives," in the language of the day, since they were used to hard work and could more easily go back where they had come from when business was slack. But the success of manufacturing in New Hampshire—particularly in the years following the Civil War—led mill owners to rely on a growing number of foreign immigrants to the state. By the 1890s, one out of every five New Hampshire residents was foreign-born. Irish, southern European and Slavic workers came to answer the morning whistles in the factory towns, but the vast majority of the immigrants were French Canadian. In the country villages of Quebec, handbills were posted to advertise the advantages of a weekly wage in Manchester or Nashua; employers chartered trains and shipped entire French families south to tend the power looms and shoe-stitching machines. In the bedrock towns of Yankee Congregationalism, the Church of Rome came to stay.

As industry advanced in 19th-century New Hampshire, agriculture went into retreat. The crumbling stone walls in what are now deep woods tell of pastures abandoned a hundred years ago and more, as farmers moved west to the more fertile prairies, or resettled after serving in the Civil War. Although the Civil War's influence was more acutely felt in Vermont, the California Gold Rush of 1849 also drew New Hampshire farmers from their land. Whether it was due to the pull of local factories or the temptation to migrate westward, the result was the same: the hill farms went fallow, and the "golden age of rural life" was over.

Another great influence on the character of 19th-century life in New Hampshire was the railroad. The iron horse first penetrated the Granite State by way of the Merrimack Valley, along a line built between Lowell, Massachusetts and Nashua in 1838. The tracks reached Concord four years later, giving the valley its potent combination of water power for industry and steam traction for

## The 19th Century: Industrial New Hampshire

The New Hampshire writer Ella Shannon Bowles once noted that the 50 years following the American Revolution were "the golden age of rural life" in her state. So it must have been, not only for New Hampshire but also for all New England. The era of back-country Indian raids was over, and the amount of cleared and cultivated land was approaching its maximum percentage of the region's total area. In 1830, 83 percent of New Hampshire's citizens were farmers. But even as the state seemed to personify the Jeffersonian ideal of a commonwealth of husbandmen, radical changes were in the offing. Benjamin Prichard's first mill at New Ipswich was the harbinger of an entirely new approach to the use of New Hampshire's resources.

By 1810 there were 12 cotton mills in New Hampshire; by 1832, 40. The first power loom appeared at Manchester's Amoskeag Mills in 1819. Four years later, Allan Sawyer established a factory at Weare that was soon turning out 20,000 pairs of shoes annually. Operations such as Sawyer's, which was followed by three other shoe factories at Farmington, Rochester and Dover, served to accomplish two things. First, they centralized pro-

transportation. At midcentury, the Boston & Maine reached Exeter and Dover, and soon began to swallow the smaller companies that had extended lines to Portsmouth and up through the Lakes region and Connecticut Valley. By the 1870s, even the White Mountains had been breached by way of Crawford Notch, and the great age of the mountain resort hotels had begun. North of the White Mountains, the Grand Trunk Railway crossed New Hampshire along its route between Montreal and Portland, Maine. As everywhere in the America of the latter 1800s, the effect of all this railroad building was to consolidate the hold of the cities on the economy, and to break down the barriers between urban and rural places in a way Governor John Wentworth could only have dreamed of with his roughly-hewn road system.

The third important theme in the 19th century development of New Hampshire was the exploitation of the northern forests. Although men had been logging in the hills of Coös County since 1825, it wasn't until after the Civil War that the timber industry came to the North Country on a grand scale. With an increasingly literate population and a newly-mechanized printing industry, the demand for paper in the America of that era was growing rapidly, and paper was what northern New Hampshire's vast softwood forests could provide. The growth of the forest products industry in this far corner of the state was partly the result of the Berlin Mills Company consolidating more than 350,000 acres of land under single ownership (including tracts in Maine and New Hampshire) by 1900, and the firm's establishing of pulp mills in the timber capital of Berlin; but the use of narrow-gauge logging railroads also played a vital role. Nevertheless, the traditional "river drive" remained an important means of getting logs to the mills well into this century.

During the colonial period and in the early years of independence, New Hampshire sought much of its wealth upon the sea. But whether they drove logs up north or mill wheels in the southern valleys, it was the inland waterways of the state that generated its prosperity as the modern era approached.

*Above:* In the 1920s, as today, pulpwood was the bread-and-butter crop of the North Country. Every log in this vast pile descended the Androscoggin River to the insatiable maw of the Brown Company mills at Berlin. *Left:* Downtown Berlin early in the 20th century.

*Facing page, top:* A view of Manchester in its late adolescence, around the middle of the last century. During the generation that followed, the city grew to become the world's largest producer of cotton cloth. *Bottom:* When the Portland and Ogdensburg Railroad conquered the grades and ravines of Crawford Notch in the early 1870s, the stage was set for the glory days of White Mountains tourism. In this Kilburn stereoscope view, a train crosses the Willy Brook Trestle.
IMAGES COURTESY NEW HAMPSHIRE HISTORICAL SOCIETY

*Above: A summer morning on the porch at the Maplewood, grandest of Bethlehem's mountain resort hotels. The time is the 1890s, when a gentleman wore a hat; we can't imagine what had come over the fellow turning to face the camera at left center.* COURTESY NEW HAMPSHIRE HISTORICAL SOCIETY

*Facing page: Rotting ties still mark the right-of-way of this abandoned logging railroad along the East Branch of the Pemigewasset River.* GEORGE WUERTHNER

## Making of Contemporary New Hampshire

Anyone who had looked even casually at New Hampshire in the year 1900 would have realized that the development of centralized industries and the railroad had combined to create a place far different from the farming and seafaring state of a century earlier. But if an observer were to suppose that the job was finished—an easy conclusion in the face of such granite certainties as the Amoskeag mills and the Boston & Maine—he would be far off the mark. New Hampshire was to change just as drastically during the 20th century as it had in the 19th. And in many aspects of economic and social development, things would get worse before they got better.

For the first few decades after the turn of the century, the Amoskeag Manufacturing Company of Manchester seemed as though it would go on spinning and weaving cotton forever. But after a hundred years of growth, the end came swiftly: a devastating strike in 1922, followed by a decade during which management decided that the growing competitiveness of the non-unionized southern states was a thing better invested in than fought, led to the giant firm's closing in 1935. Suddenly almost 11,000 of Manchester's citizens were out of work, making for a depression-within-the-Depression in New Hampshire's largest city. Throughout the state, the scenario was repeated in scores of smaller textile mills. The shoe industry, that other pillar of manufacturing prowess along the Merrimack Valley, survived somewhat longer. But in the post-World War II era, foreign competition finished off one after another of the shoe factories just as the cheaper labor and more modern plants of the South had undermined the New England textile business.

The railroad turned out to be another short-lived monolith. The Boston & Maine achieved a virtual monopoly in New Hampshire during the 1890s, but steadily lost ground to cars, trucks and buses throughout the first half of the 20th century. By the early 1970s, it was bankrupt, although it has since been reorganized and combined with other tottering roads to form a regional transportation conglomerate.

But the story of modern New Hampshire was not to be a tale of gradual deindustrialization. For one thing, there were too many people—roughly half a million at the time Amoskeag closed and more than a million today—for all of them to go back to the farm; for another, there were hardly enough farms for them to go back to. What had to be accomplished was a re-diversification of the New Hampshire economy and a new specialization in products unheard of in the days when regional prosperity was based on cotton and shoe leather. These changes have really been brought about only in the past 30 years. The manufacturing environment of present-day New Hampshire is a mix of firms producing electronic circuitry and communications equipment, specialty metals, chemicals, rubber and plastic components for automobiles and microprocessors; combined with this new wave are tenacious survivors in the paper, packaging, machine tool, quarrying, textile and shoe industries.

The southern part of New Hampshire, where most of the new industrial and service-economy activity is taking place, has changed drastically over the past few decades. The men and women who tended the looms at Amoskeag lived, worked, shopped and spent what scant leisure time they had within a trolley ride of the mills. Today's electronics technicians and systems analysts live in rapidly-suburbanizing rural areas, shop in big regional malls, and tow their boats up to Lake Winnipesaukee. Theirs is a far different New Hampshire from that of the Connecticut Valley farmers or the townspeople of far northern Coös County. It has often been alleged, during the past 10 years or so, that New Hampshire is becoming two states: a relatively prosperous and diversified southern tier and a chronically depressed north country, where natives depend upon seasonal employment and low-paying jobs in the tourist-oriented service economy.

Tourism itself is an enormously important industry in today's New Hampshire, and it has changed markedly since the days when wealthy families would arrive with steamer trunks to spend entire summers at the big hotels in the White Mountains. Today skiing, autumn foliage, hiking, boating and other attractions bring far greater numbers of people to the lakes region and the mountains, although for shorter periods of time. Those who stay longer often do so on their own premises: the condominium business in central and northern New Hampshire has been as brisk as anywhere in the Northeast. Some might say the condo dwellers constitute a "third state" within New Hampshire and the one least connected to any sense of a common past.

Perhaps New Hampshire has become two or three states; depending on whom you talk to, you may hear that it's evolved into a half-dozen or more. If we take Robert Frost at his word, in these hills and valleys there is just "one each of everything," so we shouldn't be surprised if the state doesn't seem or sound the same throughout. We can only look and listen.

# CHAPTER TWO

# The Seacoast

**Right:** *An early autumn sunrise at Portsmouth.*

**Facing page:** *Aside from an outboard motor or two, there's very little in this Portsmouth view to suggest the passage of the last two centuries. Today's working harbor is on the other side of town, slightly farther up the Piscataqua.*
TOM BEAN PHOTOS

At either side of the entry to the Portsmouth Athenaeum, the delicate yet grandly-proportioned late Georgian private library that dominates Market Square a few blocks from the city's harbor, there stands a small naval cannon mounted on end. They were brought here in 1817, four years after they were captured from the British by Commodore Oliver Hazard Perry during the Battle of Lake Erie. The cannon grace the library entrance the way a pair of tusks might stand sentry at the salon of a Victorian explorer. Perry's prizes are not merely decorative, they are emblematic: this is a seafaring town, a proud town that fought for independence with vessels of its own making. Portsmouth was a builder of ships, and a builder of fortunes.

Portsmouth is the undisputed capital of the New Hampshire seacoast, that small knob of land at the state's southeastern corner whose rivers flow eastward into the Atlantic rather than west and south into the basin of the Merrimack. These rivers, which come together to form the nearly landlocked pocket of salt water called Great Bay, were the first avenues of exploration into the New Hampshire interior, and also the first outlets for the timber that soon became the colony's staple crop.

A good deal of that timber found its way to England and the shipyards of the Royal Navy, but it wasn't long before Portsmouth itself was an important shipbuilding center. Merchant and fishing vessels came first, but in 1690 the first man o' war slid down the ways into the mouth of the Piscataqua. This was the beginning of a tradition that was to last into the 1960s, when the last keels were laid at the Portsmouth Naval Shipyard. (The shipyard, actually located across the harbor in Kittery, Maine, survives today as an important naval maintenance facility. To passersby on the harbor bridges, though, its salient feature is the massive white naval prison that occupies the heights above the river's mouth. This is the largest brig on the East Coast.) Surely the greatest days of the naval shipyard came during World War II, when a new submarine was launched here every two weeks. The battle of the Atlantic was, in large part, won in Portsmouth harbor.

During Portsmouth's halcyon years of shipbuilding, though, it was the merchantmen that made the city's economy and gave it the character it has so carefully burnished and preserved. During the mid-1700s, Portsmouth's yards were averaging 25 ships per year; a hundred years later, 10 new vessels were built annually—but they were larger and faster ships including more than 30 of the peerless Yankee clippers. Humbler craft also were important to the local economy, as not all commerce was conducted on the high seas.

Back before the railroads took over, Portsmouth's link with Dover, Durham, Newmarket, Newfields and the other towns along Great Bay and its feeder rivers was the gundalow. Gundalows were flat-bottomed barge-like boats that could be sailed or poled along shallow inland waters carrying cargoes of produce, animal fodder and building materials—hardly the stuff of romance, but the commercial glue that held seacoast and hinterlands together.

*Small boat exhibit at Strawbery Banke in Portsmouth.*
HANSON CARROLL

In 1982, nearly 100 years after the last working gundalows nosed serenely through the salt marshes back of Portsmouth, a full-scale reproduction of one of the boats was launched in Portsmouth Harbor near the Strawbery Banke restoration—a fitting nautical companion to Strawbery Banke's splendid collection of 17th and 18th century structures. Strawbery Banke, a 10-acre property bordered by Marcy, Court, Washington and Hancock streets near the waterfront, is Portsmouth's answer to Colonial Williamsburg. It is nothing less than the core of the colonial town, woefully run down by the end of the last century

and very nearly lost to the bulldozers and wrecking balls of 1950s-style "urban renewal." As it happened, a group of influential Portsmouth residents convinced the authorities that the city might capitalize on the history and architecture of its oldest section rather than tear it down. The "renewal" funds were used to renew what was already here, rather than destroy and replace it. The entire area was then rechristened with the original spelling of the name given to the harbor shore by the first settlers, who found an abundance of wild strawberries growing here. Today's visitor to Strawbery Banke can enter many of the site's 35 restored houses, ranging from gracious Georgian mansions to the modest homes of small tradesmen. There also are artisans' shops, where colonial-era crafts are demonstrated. A single admission is charged, and the properties are open between May 1 and the beginning of October.

At any time of year—perhaps most of all on a winter afternoon when woodsmoke curls from the chimney pots—it is fine to wander through the tight little warren of streets between Strawbery Banke and Little Harbor. This is a narrow, peninsular part of Portsmouth, where smartly-painted, ancient wooden houses stand close together, some holding each other up for the better part of three centuries. Nearby on Pleasant Street there are grander 18th-century homes, none so lovely as the Governor John Langdon House. When he visited the five-year-old Georgian mansion in 1789, George Washington proclaimed it the "handsomest house in Portsmouth."

Governor Langdon's Portsmouth seat has plenty of competition for that title. The 1760 Wentworth-Gardner House boasts a perfect location facing the formal gardens of Prescott Park, near the harbor, as well as impeccable Georgian architecture. The Moffatt-Ladd House, on Market Street, is another Georgian gem with magnificent gardens of its own.

Not long after the Langdon House was built, the new style now called "Federal" or "Federalist" began to develop. Federal architecture is characterized by a deceptive, almost boxlike simplicity in its basic lineaments, relieved by deft proportioning of windows and doors—the windows of the

top floor in a Federal house are smaller, to eliminate any sense of topheaviness—and a chaste, reserved application of ornament that lends an air of serene elegance. Examples of the Federal style in Portsmouth are too numerous to catalogue here; they include not only freestanding mansions such as the Rundlett-May House on Middle Street but also delightful, almost toylike strings of brick rowhouses like those that line Sheafe Street off Penhallow Street, right downtown. Portsmouth's Federal homes are relics of the city's late golden age, just prior to the War of 1812; taken together with the surviving Georgian and

earlier structures, they define a city of shipwrights and chandlers, middlemen and merchant princes grown snug around their harbor.

The fact that so much is left of old Portsmouth is testimony not just to its one-time prosperity but also to the long years during which its economy was less than vibrant. Nothing was torn down, because there was little reason to put anything up. The story is a familiar one throughout New England, and suggests one reason for Bernard DeVoto's having called the region a "finished place"—not doomed, necessarily, but completed—more than 50 years ago. By the time

**Above:** *The busy wharves and downtown streets of Portsmouth, as depicted in an 1877 "bird's eye view" by Albert Ruger.* COURTESY NEW HAMPSHIRE HISTORICAL SOCIETY
**Left:** *The Aldrich House at Strawbery Banke. This was the childhood home of Thomas Bailey Aldrich, author of* The Story of a Bad Boy. ROBERT PERRON

35

the wheels of commerce began to turn again in coastal New Hampshire, the ethic of preservation was strong enough to ensure that fine old buildings would be restored for new purposes, rather than demolished in the name of progress. We've seen this with regard to Strawbery Banke, which has become a living museum. But much of Portsmouth's venerable brick and mortar has been transformed into offices, boutiques, apartments, condominiums and an incredible variety of restaurants. You can eat Yankee, French, Japanese, Szechuan, Mexican or Greek food here in surroundings ranging from old waterfront countinghouses to a rehabbed church. It's the classic 1960s-through-1980s gentrification story, but with a happy twist: Portsmouth is large enough, and so far eclectic enough, to enable hardware stores, cheap little bistros and used-book shops to survive cheek-by-jowl with *nouvelle cuisine* and art glass. The place hasn't become a homogenized tourist town. It has texture and depth, Portsmouth does.

## New Hampshire's Seacoast Resorts

Compared to its neighbors, Maine and Massachusetts, New Hampshire has never enjoyed a wide reputation as a seacoast resort state. The reason is obvious—by the time colonial politicians in London, Portsmouth and Boston had finished their wranglings, the state was left with a scant 18 miles of ocean frontage. There is no Hyannis or Ogunquit here, no Provincetown nor even an Old Orchard Beach. Although sandy beaches at Hampton and Rye interrupt the rocky coast, a charitable description of the water temperature might be "brisk." Still, New Hampshire's coast has its summer partisans, even if many of them would rather bathe in the sun than in the sea.

If you're heading south from Portsmouth, the quickest way through the coastal towns to Massachusetts is Route 1—but it is hardly the most scenic. Far better to press along the alternate routes that hug the coast, beginning with Route 1B as it loops through the old settlement of New Castle, actually an island connected to the mainland by bridges. This is where New Hampshiremen staged their famous raid on Fort William and Mary in December 1774, presaging the revolutionary battles of the following spring. Rebuilt in 1808 and renamed Fort Constitution, the old garrison still stands. Many of the saltbox-style fishermen's houses that cluster along New Castle's winding lanes were here well before Fort William and Mary fell, and have a look about them that suggests they will survive another century or two. The grandest structure on the island, though, is a relative newcomer. This is the Wentworth Hotel, a vast Victorian ark that once hosted delegates to the 1905 peace conference that produced the Treaty of Portsmouth and ended the Russo-Japanese War. Long empty, it now faces a new life as a condominium development.

South of New Castle, at the northern tip of New Hampshire's mainland coast where Route 1A begins its short, salt-sprayed run towards Massachusetts, the promontory called Odiorne's Point is the focus of one of New Hampshire's loveliest parks. Here is where Samuel de Champlain and John Smith first took measure of the New Hampshire coast, and where David Thomson and his party built their trading post—the colony's first settlement—in 1623. But today's visitor to Odiorne's Point is immediately put in mind of much more recent events, as the site is still dotted with the remnants of observation bunkers and gun turrets built during World War II. Odiorne's Point

*Above:* A salt marsh near Rye Beach. Salt marshes now are recognized as important flood-protection mechanisms, and as the vital primary link in the marine food chain. GEORGE WUERTHNER *Left:* Fort Constitution, at New Castle, once guarded the approach to Portsmouth Harbor. As Fort William and Mary, it was the site of the first rebel action against the British military presence. CLYDE H. SMITH

*Facing page, right:* Tugs at anchor, Portsmouth harbor. This is the view from a number of chic downtown restaurants and taverns. NONA BAUER *Top:* Colored wooden buoys mark where lobster "pots" rest on the ocean floor. Lobstering still is an important industry, despite declining stock. TOM BEAN *Bottom:* Live free or die: A New Hampshireman can decorate his storefront any way he pleases. NONA BAUER

was the closest line of defense for the great shipbuilding city to the north, and a good place to watch for submarines launched not in Portsmouth but in Bremerhaven. Today the point is a peaceful, grassy bluff above the ocean, and as fine a spot for a picnic as any on New Hampshire's short seaboard.

From Odiorne's Point south, Route 1A is the kind of road you always dream of traveling in the right car, with no one else around. The blacktop dips and turns along the crest of the rocky cliffs that mark the shore, past turn-of-the-century mansions on Little Boar's Head (one is the governor's official summer residence) and placid expanses of marshland. The character of this seaside drive quickly changes, though, when you reach Hampton Beach.

Hampton Beach is a throwback to an earlier species of oceanside resort. There's nothing the slightest bit chic about it; it is very much a place of blue-collar summer rentals and arcades on the strip. On one side of Route 1A is a long boardwalk, with steps leading down to the broad strand of the Hampton Beach State Reservation. On the other side is a Smithsonian-quality slice of beachfront Americana: seafood restaurants, ice cream stands, video games, small hotels (though not nearly so many as the 200 that lined the main drag and back streets 50 years ago), bars and Hampton Beach's biggest building, the old wooden Casino. The Hampton Beach Casino runs one of the seacoast's most ambitious pop concert programs each year, and if you are trying to inch your car through town as an Emmylou Harris show lets out, you may as well park for a while and take a walk on the beach.

*Left: Summer homes at Hampton Beach are a bit more modest than their counterparts at Rye.* CHRISTIAN HEEB
***Facing page, left:*** *The main drag at Hampton Beach. Had this been a summer day, the foreground would have been a creeping wall of Detroit iron.* GEORGE WUERTHNER ***Right:*** *An aerial civew of Portsmouth.* CLYDE H. SMITH

## Heading Inland

There is more to Hampton than Hampton Beach, just as there is more to the entire seacoast region than the towns that cluster directly on the ocean between Portsmouth and the Massachusetts line. If you drive due west along the roads that lead from 1A inland past Interstate 95, it's easy to lose any sense of the sea being nearby. The rolling hills beyond the ugly commercial strip of Route 1 are semirural, and in fact agriculture survives here on a surprisingly large scale in the form of Hampton Falls' Applecrest Farms. Applecrest may seem like just another farmstand to the casual shopper, but out back are over 10,000 trees on land that might have been a developer's dream.

Two of coastal New Hampshire's towns boast education as their principal industry. Exeter is the home of Phillips Exeter Academy, founded in 1783 by wealthy Exeter merchant John Phillips and today occupying a handsome neo-Georgian campus a few blocks from the center of the compact and attractive town. Today one of the nation's preeminent college preparatory schools (as is its cousin, Phillips Academy in Andover, Massachusetts), Exeter counts among its alumni the sons of Presidents Lincoln, Grant and Cleveland. Daniel Webster studied here for nine months, as part of his preparation for Dartmouth College.

Farther north, at the head of a tidal arm of Great Bay called Oyster River, the old shipbuilding town of Durham is the seat of the University of New Hampshire. This wasn't always so; UNH began as a state agricultural college, established in 1866 and located in the shadow of Dartmouth at Hanover. Never prosperous or well attended throughout its quarter-century as Dartmouth's farm-oriented poor relation, the college was moved clear across the state to Durham in 1891 and slowly allowed to broaden its curriculum. As a university after 1923, UNH placed liberal arts on an equal footing with agriculture. Today, more than 10,000 students are enrolled at the Durham campus in undergraduate and graduate programs.

## The Isles of Shoals

One of those UNH programs, in marine biology, is headquartered during summer at a place barely nine miles from Portsmouth harbor,

*Hampton Beach harbor at sunset.* PHILIP KEENAN

ered" by Captain John Smith in 1614, but it is likely that Spanish, Portuguese and Basque fishermen were using them as cod-drying stations even before the venturesome Englishman honored them with his own name. In any event, the era of colonial settlement that followed Smith's explorations saw hundreds of fishermen come to live on the Isles of Shoals, sensibly renamed because of the way fish "shoaled" or schooled in their vicinity. During the late 18th century the little colony began to diminish because of overfishing, and by the middle of the 1800s only a few reclusive types remained upon these barren rocks with the cormorants and gulls.

One seclusion-seeking mainlander who packed up and headed for the Isles of Shoals was Thomas Laighton. He arrived with his family on White Island in 1839, at first serving as lighthouse keeper but later opening a hotel on Appledore to cater to the summer tourist trade. His daughter, Celia Laighton Thaxter (1835-1894), identified so strongly with the place of her upbringing that she returned to a cottage on Appledore each summer throughout her adult life, and made the Isles the subject of much of her popular verse and her prose account *Among the Isles of Shoals*. More than her home and inspiration, Appledore was the site of Celia Thaxter's famous literary salons, which were attended by the likes of Whittier, Emerson, Lowell and the elder Oliver Wendell Holmes. The Isles' laureate is buried on Appledore, not far from the site of her cottage.

Thomas Laighton's hotel on Appledore burned more than 70 years ago, but the isles' other great hostelry, the Oceanic on Star Island, has survived to this day as the center for a lively program of summer conferences. These are the week-long sessions held under the auspices of the Star Island Corporation, ranging from religious retreats (the Corporation is loosely affiliated with the Unitarian-Universalist Church) to a secular "Conference on the Arts" that includes areas as varied as painting, dance, writing, theater and photography. I once had the opportunity to teach a non-fiction workshop as part of an arts conference, and believe I can speak for my students and fellow instructors in suggesting that simply being

yet as isolated as any spot in New England. This is Appledore Island, one of the Isles of Shoals off the New Hampshire coast. Along with Smuttynose, Duck, Cedar and Malaga Islands, Appledore is technically a part of Kittery, Maine. But the town of Rye, New Hampshire can claim White Island, once the home of the Isles' most famous resident; and Star Island, the isle most frequently visited today.

The rocky and virtually treeless Isles of Shoals offered the first experience modern Europeans had of the New Hampshire coast. (The term "modern" will protect us from the shades of Dr. Barry Fell's ancient Celts.) They were "discov-

on Star Island was as important as what we were doing there. "You will come back" is the traditional chant of the Star Island staff as the boat for Portsmouth leaves with its complement of departing conferees, and although it hasn't happened yet, I have to confess an occasional strong desire to spend an hour or two in a broad-armed rocker on the verandah of the old Oceanic, contemplating nothing and surrounded by the sweet desolation of the Isles of Shoals. Celia Thaxter knew what she was about.

The serenity of the Isles of Shoals was almost lost, in 1973, when Aristotle Onassis's scheme to build an enormous oil refinery at Durham, with a companion supertanker port at the Isles, was

given the enthusiastic support of New Hampshire Governor Meldrim Thomson. Even if never a drop of oil had been spilled, the operation would have irrevocably changed the character of the islands—to say nothing of collegiate Durham. It was the citizenry of that community who shut the door on Onassis and his plan by voting down the refinery at the following spring's town meeting.

## Seabrook and the Question of Nuclear Power

Depending on what side you take in New Hampshire's biggest political controversy of this century, you might argue that the people of Seabrook, on the seacoast's Massachusetts border, have not been so lucky as those who care about

***Above:*** *A farmstand in Wilton. As in the rest of New England, farms stay alive by diversifying and opening retail stands to offer locally-grown produce.*
GEORGE WUERTHNER

***Left:*** *The old Oceanic Hotel dominates this aerial view of Star Island, one of the Isles of Shoals off the New Hampshire coast. Each summer, the hotel and surrounding cottages fill with participants in religious and arts conferences.* CLYDE H. SMITH

*The controversial Seabrook nuclear power station.*
GEORGE WUERTHNER

choice of location was Newington, but the U.S. Air Force objected that a Newington plant would be too close to the runways at Pease Air Force Base. The decision was made to build the two-reactor project at Seabrook, on a stretch of marshland just north of the Massachusetts border. It had to be built somewhere, Public Service maintained; the region needed the electricity. Others argued—and still do—that conservation is the answer, and that the utility's regional growth estimates always have been way off the mark.

With construction of Seabrook Station already under way, the town's residents voted in March 1976, by a ratio of approximately seven to six, that they did not want the plant within their borders. The Public Service Company had greater influence in state government than Aristotle Onassis, though, and this time the town meeting vote did not close the issue. Frustration with what was perceived as the circumvention of political and regulatory processes soon led to the radicalizing of Seabrook's most vocal opponents. The confrontation-style politics of the Vietnam era soon came to the fore, and a coalition of antinuclear activists called the Clamshell Alliance began leading increasingly larger demonstrations at the Seabrook construction site.

Richard Cushing, a carpenter by trade who lives in Seabrook and represents the town as a Democratic member of the New Hampshire House of Representatives, helped found Clamshell in July 1976. "My original grounds for opposition had to do with environmental impact on the clam flats, back when the company was proposing a system of cooling canals," Cushing recalls. "In 1972, I went up to Portsmouth for a site evaluation committee hearing. I saw the public's testimony virtually ignored while Public Service's consultants got all the attention, and my frustration turned to rage." Four years later, when the demonstrations began, Cushing was in the thick of things. He was arrested twice during the summer of 1976, when the first groups of protesters walked down the old B&M tracks from Hampton Falls to stage sit-ins at the plant site, and again at the biggest antiSeabrook demonstration of all, on April 30, 1977. That was the day the seacoast's anti-nuclear

the Isles of Shoals. "Seabrook," before 1976, was simply the name of a small town on Route 1, and of its mini-Hampton oceanfront strip across the salt marshes. Next it became the name of a pair of nuclear electrical generating plants. Now it is the crux and summation of the entire nuclear power issue in New England, and a word that raises hackles far beyond the region's boundaries.

The Seabrook nuclear story began in 1968, when Public Service of New Hampshire, the state's major electric utility, first proposed building a nuclear generating facility. The company's initial

movement made news around the world, as 1,000 people were arrested, to spend the next two weeks in five National Guard armories hastily converted into detention centers by order of Governor Thomson.

Work continued on Seabrook Station throughout the decade that followed, with opposition centering increasingly upon the perceived inadequacy of emergency evacuation plans, the quality of the plant's construction, and the question of what to do with nuclear waste. With expenses and opposition piling up, work on the Unit 2 reactor was suspended in the early 1980s; Unit l, completed by 1986, as of this writing still awaits approval of evacuation plans and licensing by the Nuclear Regulatory Commission. Meanwhile, Public Service of New Hampshire is in reorganization, having filed for bankruptcy protection in the wake of its mammoth but as yet unremunerative investment in nuclear power.

Richard Cushing, his anger simply channeled rather than diminished now that he spends his days at the State House in Concord, regrets none of the extralegal confrontations of which he was a part in the 1970s. "The system failed people, and forced direct action," he argues. "The first demonstrations were in support of the town's vote against the plant. Public Service went all out to sway the voters and lost—and then they didn't respect that position. It's important to remember that the original resistance to Seabrook was local. The early opposition wasn't fomented by outsiders, but by fishermen, clammers—conservative Yankee Republicans." Elected in 1986 to a legislature traditionally dominated by politicians of just that stamp, Cushing has worked to support legislation that will prevent Seabrook Station from operating. One resolution he successfully backed put the House on record against a utility-proposed reduction of the 10-mile evacuation zone; a bill he introduced, to ban the dumping of chlorine in waterways as plant operation would require, did not pass. But whether the battles are won or lost, Cushing is confident about the war: "I used to say if we knew how victory would finally come about, we'd have already won...but my feeling is that we will create a political climate which will make

Seabrook impossible to operate as a nuclear plant. We're going to win. We have to win. I don't even want to contemplate failure." If the 400 men and women who meet in Concord are indeed a "citizens' legislature," Robert Cushing is its quintessence; if they can be moved to accomplishments beyond the power of town meeting, he bids fair to do the moving—or Molly Stark's a widow.

*Tourism may be big business, but the spiritual background of a seacoast economy is commercial fishing. This fish handler at Portsmouth is part of a line that dates back beyond the first English settlers to the peripatetic Bretons and Basques.* CLYDE H. SMITH

# CHAPTER THREE

# The Merrimack Valley

**Right:** *The boulder-strewn Pemigewasset River, north of the point where it meets the Winnipesaukee to form the Merrimack.* CLYDE H. SMITH

**Facing page:** *An apple orchard at Hollis.* NONA BAUER

In the spring of the year meltwater from the White Mountains runs cold and fast, collecting in nameless rivulets that feed the tributary branches of the Pemigewasset River in the vast wilderness south of Franconia Notch. The Pemigewasset proper begins in the town of Woodstock, and gathers force as it drops south past Plymouth and Bristol toward Franklin Falls. In the old mill town of Franklin, just below the falls, the Pemigewasset meets the Winnipesaukee River, fresh out of Winnisquam Lake. At their confluence the two rivers take a new name: Merrimack, "swift water" in the language of the Penacooks. From here on, throughout its 60-mile descent to the Massachusetts border, the Merrimack is the determining fact of New Hampshire, its Nile and its Rhine. Neither here nor along its final course through Massachusetts is it needed any longer as a means of transportation or a major source of power, but the string of cities it created during the Industrial Revolution are still the region's main centers of population and commerce. Southern New Hampshire is built around the Merrimack River.

We can travel the whole of the Pemigewasset/Merrimack Valley today and find that nowhere, except at the swollen stretch above the Franklin Falls dam, does the river reach lake-like proportions. But as the last of the glaciers receded some 12,000 years ago, a broad body of water called Lake Merrimack extended from modern-day Plymouth, near Squam Lake, down to Lowell, Massachusetts, where the Merrimack River now begins its sharp northeastward arc toward tidewater at Newburyport. (The Bay State now has the lower Merrimack because of an 18th-century agreement that set the New Hampshire border three miles north of the river roughly from Lowell to the sea.) The great lake was fed the way the wilderness feeder streams of the Merrimack are fed today, by melting ice and snow, but on such a grand scale and at such a stately pace that it took 500 years for the inland sea of meltwater to extend the 20 miles from Concord north to Franklin. At last relieved of the glacier's awful weight, the surface of New Hampshire rose and tipped the shallow lake into the Atlantic. What remained was the ancient river, its drainage slowly cutting down

through layers of outwash clay. "Varved" clay, geologists call it, and each varve, or laminated band of sediment, records the annual retreat of the glacier like the rings in a stump chronicle the growth of a tree.

The Algonquian tribes who settled in the Merrimack Valley found the river an ideal highway for their bark canoes—or rather, they evolved the exquisite form of the canoe in precise response to the character of rivers like the Ammonoosuc and the Androscoggin, the Pemigewasset and the Merrimack. Certainly the forests provided plenty of birch trees from which the Indians could make their boats—not the reedy young birches that we know today, but stout old trees yielding bark capable of covering the frame of a big canoe, and as important to the migratory tribes as the mast pines later were to the Royal Navy.

The Merrimack and its tributaries were a vital source of food as well as an important transporta-

tion network. Now that pollution has abated sufficiently for Atlantic salmon to return to some of their historic spawning streams, their numbers are so small that each mile of penetration past tidewater is heralded as an accomplishment; biologists must hardly know whether to tag them or give them Christian names. But in the days before white men built their dams and mills, and muddied the streams with soil eroded from clear-cut hillsides, the annual runs of salmon and shad were prodigious. In the Salmon Falls River, which forms the southern boundary between New Hampshire and Maine, salmon were once so thick at spawning time that the story was told of how the Indians walked from shore to shore upon the fishes' backs. Though surely apocryphal, tales like these tell something of the piscine abundance New Hampshire's rivers once offered. The Merrimack, in season, was once alive with salmon, shad, alewives, eels and other fish.

*Above:* *The village church at Amherst. Just east of the church stood the courthouse (since moved to another location in town) where a young lawyer named Daniel Webster made his first plea, in 1805.*
*Right:* *Welcome on a winter's night: Fitzwilliam.*
CLYDE H. SMITH PHOTOS

*Facing page:* *A 1968 view of the Amoskeag Mills, Manchester, by architectural conservator Randolph Langenbach. Since this was taken, the canal in the foreground and all buildings except the one with the tower have been demolished.* RANDOLPH LANGENBACH

The English colonists found the Merrimack as handy a road into the New Hampshire interior as the Indians had, but prior to the middle of the 18th century it was a road they often found it wise to avoid—at least as a path to permanent settlement. Although Chief Wonalancet had led many of the Penacooks into Canada by 1700, French-incited raids along the Merrimack Valley persisted into the 1750s. Settlements on the sites of Manchester and Concord were not made until the 1720s; farther north, Franklin was not settled until 1764. But in the years immediately prior to the Revolution, the valley began to fill quickly. Soon the Merrimack was dotted with the colonists' flatboats,

carrying staples such as salt, rum and iron to the little towns, and bringing timber and harvested crops to the cities of the coast.

Among the earliest settlers to brave the dangers of the Merrimack Valley and the lands beyond were Scotch-Irish immigrants, who came to New Hampshire by way of Northern Ireland. The first foothold of the Scots was Londonderry, settled in 1719; soon they so predominated in the farms and village around the Amoskeag Falls that in 1751 this future site of Manchester was chartered as "Derryfield." Along with their uncompromising Presbyterian brand of Calvinism they brought America its first potatoes, as well as their talent for the cultivation and spinning of flax. By 1766, the farmers and cottage weavers of the lower Merrimack Valley towns were turning out 25,000 yards of linen each year. This may seem a pittance when we reflect that the Manchester power looms of a century and a half later could equal this output (in cotton) in barely a quarter of an hour, but the Derry crofters were working entirely by hand. Their industriousness was a portent for the Merrimack Valley.

And so the Scots wove themselves into the fabric of New Hampshire, though never so completely as not to stand out proudly for what they are. I met an old gentleman one day in the rotunda of the New Hampshire Historical Society building in Concord. He was a New Hampshire Yankee to the bone, a member of the Historical Society as well as of the Sons of the American Revolution. But he was nonetheless a Scot, though removed from the homeland by seven generations in the New World and at least two or three before that in Northern Ireland. He wore a bright tartan sport jacket, and despite his impeccable S.A.R. credentials he spoke proudly of his Nova Scotia ancestors, originally from New Hampshire. "They were Tories," he told me. "Some of them fought against the Continental Army in the Seventy-eighth Highland Regiment. When the war was over, they went to Canada." "The war"—he tossed off the words as if he were speaking of World War II, or Vietnam. Here was a man for whom two centuries of history is all quite recent, and who has no trouble with a spiritual sense of dual nationality. Regardless of some of his forebears' antipathy to the colonial cause, I would suspect he agrees with General Stark about living free.

The city in which the Scottish gentleman and I spoke is the capital of New Hampshire, made so by an act of the state legislature in 1808. By then the Merrimack Valley towns were comfortable and secure; only greybeards could remember the attacks of the French and Indians. By then, also, the citizens of the interior were finally numerous and powerful enough to take the seat of government from Portsmouth, and leave the old haunt of the Wentworths to the business of making money rather than laws.

*Above: The New Hampshire Capitol at Concord. Beneath the gold-leafed dome sits the largest legislature in the United States.* CLYDE H. SMITH

*Right: In the Granite State, Concord long has been the Granite City. Many of America's most famous public buildings are made of stone from Concord's quarries.* COURTESY NEW HAMPSHIRE HISTORICAL SOCIETY

*Facing page: Franklin Pierce, New Hampshire's only United States President, is portrayed on the capitol grounds.* CHRISTIAN HEEB

## Concord: Canals, Coaches and the Capital

As it happened, Concord knew how to turn a few dollars as well. By 1815, New Hampshire's capital had direct access to the port of Boston in the form of the Middlesex Canal. Actually a series of canals linking the navigable sections of the Merrimack River, the new water route had taken 20 years to complete, and included a complicated system of locks to allow passage around the wild Amoskeag Falls at Manchester. Once the project was finished, two-man crews regularly poled 75-foot canal boats on five-day trips up the waterway from Boston to Concord, and returned with the current in less than a day's time. The canal's heyday lasted only 20 years, until the railroad reached up along the Merrimack and took the traffic away. But in the meantime, the availability

of cheap transportation put Concord's fledgling industries on the map. Chief among these was quarrying: more than anything else, it was the output of Concord's quarries that earned New Hampshire its standing as the "Granite State."

Another celebrated product of New Hampshire's capital was the Concord coach. In 1813, a man named Lewis Downing established a business that would make Concord the Detroit of the stagecoach era. The Concord coaches Downing built with his partner, Stephen Abbot, were a marked improvement over earlier horse-drawn conveyances. They incorporated the revolutionary idea of leather straps, or "thoroughbraces," slung beneath each side of the body to help isolate passengers from the bumpy, rutted roads of the era. Concord coaches were known the world over, before internal combustion dealt them the same blow that steam had dealt the Middlesex Canal. There is a meticulously restored Concord coach on exhibit at the New Hampshire Historical Society. Protected and immobile in its upstairs alcove, it is instantly recognizable as the baggage-laden, strongbox-carrying, hell-for-leather chariot of a thousand Saturday matinees.

The austere classical building across the street from the Historical Society serves as the seat of the most famous "industry" in Concord's history—the government of New Hampshire. Here, in the first state to adopt an independent constitution following the outbreak of rebellion against England, the work of governing is carried on in the oldest state house in which a legislature still meets in its original chambers. New Hampshire's Capitol was built in 1819, and it is made of granite.

The Capitol's gold-leafed, octagonal dome is the first glimpse you get of Concord as you drive north into the pretty valley where the city stands. Concord never spread back very far from its original site on the west bank of the Merrimack; the Capitol itself faces the river (obscured now by brick business blocks and Interstate 93) from a landscaped block on North Main Street barely a third of a mile from the riverbanks. As befits the seat of a "citizens' legislature," as the New Hampshire House of Representatives likes to call itself, the Capitol is an open and approachable building, no more imposing for all its pillared dignity than a county courthouse in a country town. Immediately inside are the flags and faces New Hampshire has chosen to represent itself to casual visitors, or perhaps to inspire some newly-elected legislator from a remote rural district. The flags, furled and cased in glass, are those carried by New Hampshire regiments over the centuries; the faces are those of the generals and politicians the state has set before the nation. (The most famous of these are cast in bronze on the lawn outside—General John Stark, President Franklin Pierce, anti-slavery leader John Parker Hale, and the most famous New Hamp-shireman of all, a Dartmouth-trained lawyer from Salisbury named Daniel Webster.) Amongst all the stern portraits that line the hallways, two stand out. The first is that of a goodly, grey-haired lady from Bow, Mary Baker Eddy, who wrote *Science*

*and Health With Key to the Scriptures* and founded the Christian Science Church. The second is of a New Hampshire native whose approach to the heavens was more literal than metaphysical. Alan Shepard is portrayed in the full silvery regalia of his astronaut suit, and the painting is accompanied by the state flag he took to the moon and a tiny specimen of moon rock. This is about the only form of mineral a local might concede to be as valuable as a good block of Concord granite, although so far there hasn't been remotely as practical a use for the stuff.

We might reasonably expect that someday another space explorer's portrait might grace the halls of the Capitol. Christa McAuliffe was a Concord schoolteacher at the time she was chosen to represent her profession on the crew of the ill-fated space shuttle *Challenger*. In the eyes of her

fellow New Hampshire men and women, she is the nearest thing to a citizen-heroine that the state has produced in modern times.

The floors upstairs from the halls of flags and portraits are trod far more often by plain citizens than by heroes and heroines. With 400 members, the New Hampshire House of Representatives is the largest legislature in the nation, save for the only slightly larger U.S. House. This elephantine institution (it's accompanied by a 24-member Senate) is a relic of New Hampshire's earliest days as a state, and reflects a commitment to draw representatives not only from artificially-constructed districts, but also from each town with sufficient population.

A similar predilection for decentralization of authority is reflected in the fact that for a century New Hampshire governors have been limited to a

*The Hillsboro homestead of Franklin Pierce, 14th president of the United States.* GEORGE WUERTHNER

**Facing page:** *Sunrise, Lake Winnipesaukee. Three sailboats are company, but many residents of lakeside communities are beginning to wonder whether Winnipesaukee's thousands of sail and power-driven craft might not constitute a crowd.* © GARY BRAASCH

term of office lasting two years although they may be reelected to subsequent terms. The upshot of this constitutional quirk is that the actions of a chief executive's entire term are quite fresh in the voters' minds when he stands for re-election. In the unlikely event that a governor were to break his pledge and sneak through an unprecedented sales or income tax, he would have virtually no time to redeem himself before the polls opened again. To further stifle gubernatorial arrogation of power, New Hampshire's constitution remains one of three in the Union to retain the colonial institution known as the Executive Council. The Councilors, chosen by popular election, are empowered to approve or reject the governor's appointments and budgetary decisions. In Maine and Massachusetts, the Council survives but is largely ceremonial; in New Hampshire, it still is a potent

fact of political life. Taken together, the massive legislature and sharply circumscribed executive powers characteristic of New Hampshire government understandably lead an observer to wonder whether or not the citizens of the Granite State really *want* to be governed. The State House is a proud fixture for Concord and a good place to keep moon rocks, but as far as managing affairs of state…well, that can be done in March, at town meeting.

## The Mills of Manchester

New Hampshire people may not like to be governed, but for a long time many of their lives were regulated, in the Merrimack Valley, by steam whistles belonging to an institution far more powerful than any legislature that ever sat in Concord. The history of this part of the state throughout the century that ended with the Great Depression is in large part the history of the Amoskeag Manufacturing Company. Amoskeag was by no means the only company to put the waters of the Merrimack and the people of the valley to work, but it was by far the greatest. Today, more than 50 years after its closing, it still can serve as a model for explaining the entire industrial experience in New Hampshire.

Walk north along the Merrimack, toward the Amoskeag Falls at the heart of Manchester, and for two miles there will be nothing to your right but the somber brick walls of the mill buildings. They long have outlived the company that built them, largely because they have been useful for harboring any number of smaller enterprises, from discount clothing outlets to a soup factory, but at least partly because tearing down the physical reminders of Amoskeag would be too, too profound a departure from Manchester's past.

New Hampshire's largest city, after all, owes even its name to the makers of cotton cloth. It was Samuel Blodgett, the visionary whose energy had seen through the completion of the canal around the Amoskeag Falls in 1807, who pronounced that here would stand the "Manchester of America." The name was officially changed from Derryfield to Manchester just three years later, by which time Benjamin Prichard's 85 spindles already were turn-

The identification of Manchester people with the great mill was fostered not only by multigeneration employment within the same households, but also by the company's involvement in so many aspects of life outside the factory. Workers read the *Amoskeag Bulletin,* published by the company-sponsored Amoskeag Textile Club; they took English lessons from teachers engaged by the club, and even fished for trout that it stocked in local streams. They played on company sports teams and learned home economics in company classes. Although only 15 percent or so of Amoskeag's employees lived in company housing, they were citizens of a community whose City Hall was built on land donated by the firm. Whether or not the Amoskeag Manufacturing Company owned the roof over your head was a small point, really; the fact was that there would be no city, no social fabric as the workers knew it, without the omnipotent mill. Was that good or bad? Was the Amoskeag, finally, an institution ruled by enlightened self-interest or simply a "dark, satanic mill" on the most gigantic of scales? Any answer we arrive at will invariably be colored by our own politics and a sense of how we would like to have spent our days in the year 1910 if we had just dropped out of grammar school or gotten off a train from Quebec. The memories and observations of those who knew this way of living first hand are collected in a wonderful book by Tamara Hareven and Randolph Langenbach called *Amoskeag.* In it, one former mill hand comes as close as anyone is likely towards summing up the feelings of tens of thousands of his fellow workers: "You thought this was what life was all about."

The life that was the Amoskeag took a bad turn in 1922, when the company's directors applied bitter medicine to an operation hard-hit by the postwar economic slump. Wages were cut by 20 percent, while time on the job was increased by 12$^1$/$_2$—from 48 to 54 hours per week. Transferring their loyalty from the mill to the United Textile Workers, an overwhelming majority of the Amoskeag's hands went on strike. The walkout lasted nine months. When it was over, the wage cut had been rescinded but the longer hours remained. The workers' regard for the union and

its out-of-town organizers was diminished, but far more important was the community's loss of confidence in the beneficence of the Amoskeag itself. The new adversarial relationship between those who had been participants in a near-feudal arrangement set the stage for the departure of the Amoskeag from Manchester; the strike didn't kill the company, but it made the people of the Merrimack Valley realize that perhaps spinning cotton for a monolithic Boston-based firm would not always be "what life was all about."

The end, as we noted earlier, came quickly. In 1925 the Amoskeag board of directors created a holding company to which it transferred $18 million in banked profits. The manufacturing company remained a subsidiary of the new enterprise, which chose to invest its capital in other businesses (including the newer, non-unionized textile mills of the South) rather than in modernizing its physical plant along the Merrimack. The onset of

the Great Depression, followed by strikes in 1933 and 1934, spelled the end for the now-undercapitalized giant. Between March and September of 1935 the work force was reduced from 11,000 to a skeleton crew of 1,000, and later that fall the mills were shut down. Any hope of reopening was washed away in the great Merrimack River floods of the following year.

After the assets of the Amoskeag were ordered liquidated by a federal bankruptcy court in 1936, Manchester civic leaders bought the mill buildings and began to solicit new tenants. Seventeen smaller firms occupied the old giant's premises by 1938; during the years immediately following World War II, a hundred new employers were spread out in the brick buildings along the river. (Approximately 80 percent of the mill complex still is standing today.) Throughout much of the postwar era, though, industrial occupancy of the Amoskeag mills was a matter of renting

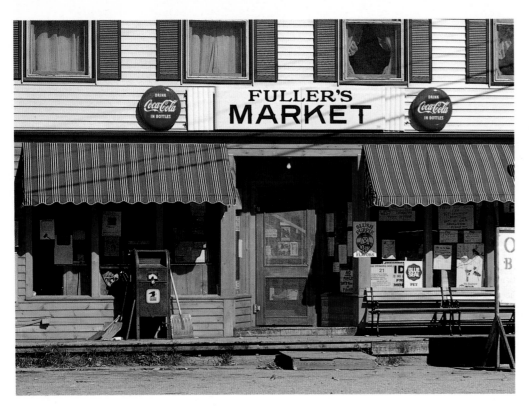

*Above:* Competition for the shopping mall, Woodstock. The mom-and-pop store that carries a little of everything is by no means extinct in New Hampshire, although benches for the town idlers are becoming more scarce. CHRISTIAN HEEB

*Right:* Rome apples, a local favorite for baking, ripe for the picking at Hollis. NONA BAUER

*Facing page:* New Hampshire has seen the future, and it is high technology. Sanders Associates headquarters, Nashua. CLYDE H. SMITH

from absentee owners, with little done in the way of building rehabilitation. This pattern was to change in the early 1980s, when entrepreneur Dean Kamen began purchasing millyard properties with an eye towards providing a home for his own medical technology research and development firm as well as leasing space to new tenants. Kamen first began thinking about the possibilities of Amoskeag's brick white elephants while looking down at Manchester during helicopter flights between his Bedford, New Hampshire home and his office in Hooksett. Appropriately, an 1875 Amoskeag building Kamen now owns is topped by a rooftop helipad—an executive perk that the masters of gingham never dreamed of.

By the end of 1987, Kamen's Deka Research and Development Corporation and its associated firms and partnerships had invested $12 million in three Amoskeag buildings totaling 550,000 square feet. The money has gone not only to initial purchase costs but also to new roofs, heating and air conditioning systems. Taken together with Deka, which specializes in developing technology for infusion pumps and life-support monitoring systems, the tenants of the modern millyard amount to an object lesson in "what life is all about" in the postindustrial Merrimack Valley: WMUR television, with the largest studio north of Boston; Teletrol Systems, specializing in energy use management by computer; Motorola Communications and Electronics; Quest Environmental Services, an environmental engineering firm; and a hands-on exhibit center for children called Science Enrichment Encounters. The list goes on, to include an advertising agency, a dance studio, a congressman's office and a restaurant.

The last of the smaller textile firms that operated in the shell of Amoskeag was gone by

1980. Manchester toils, but no longer does it spin. Who can say, though, if some lone technician, working late into the night in an electronics lab, might not hear the ghostly clangor of 24,000 looms, and an oath or two in the old Quebec patois?

Down in Nashua, where New Hampshire industry once wrung a few last kilowatts of power out of the Merrimack before the river plunged along the state line to run the mills of Lowell and Lawrence, high technology long since has replaced the shoe factories. Nashua's most important firm—and the largest private-sector employer in New Hampshire—is Sanders Associates, a Lockheed subsidiary that divides its business between electronic defense systems and computer graphic display hardware. Other high-tech players in the old shoe city include Edgcomb Steel, which processes and jobs specialty metals; Nashua Corporation, which has graduated from making waxed paper to producing computer and copying system supplies; and of course the Massachusetts-based computer giant Digital, with facilities in Nashua and other southern New Hampshire locations.

The increase in job opportunities associated with the rise of new industries in the Merrimack Valley has resulted in a dramatic upswing in the region's population and profound changes in the character of cities, towns and countryside. Between 1980 and 1986, the two southern New Hampshire counties of Rockingham and Hillsborough gained more people than any other area in New England. Nashua itself grew from 56,000 in 1970 to 68,000 in 1980 and an estimated 78,000 in 1986, and the raw numbers translate into the kind of urban pressures a city traffic engineer summed up recently by saying, "We're a little Boston up here now." Along the banks of the Nashua River, a developer has been doing a brisk business selling 484 new condominiums—and nearly one third of the buyers are from Massachusetts. Like so many camp followers come the businesses catering to sophisticated tastes: "God bless the high-tech industry," wrote a dining critic in *New England Monthly*. "It has brought southern New Hampshire prosperity, high employment, and best of all Thai food."

As cities like Nashua grow, the distinctions between urban and rural areas blur just as the dinstinction between New Hampshire and Massachusetts has blurred in an area where people drive between home and work in both directions, their commuting patterns dictated by the rise of high-tech firms along routes 3 and I-93 on both sides of the border. Since many of the people moving to southern New Hampshire are interested not only in low taxes and plentiful job opportunities but also in some vague notion of "country living," there has been a steady march of condos and single-family houses from cities out to land that was farmed just 30 years ago. A New Jersey Chamber of Commerce once coined the ugly word "ruburbia" for this sort of development, and ruburbia is what it is.

For the newcomers to the valley, the Merrimack River itself is more likely to be touted as an "amenity" nowadays than as a practical business advantage; there are only a few small hydro plants, and manufacturers don't ship semiconductors to Boston on barges. The dyehouses no longer discharge waste into the river, and—once the Environmental Protection Administration and the courts have their way—neither will the sewers of Manchester. No one will ever walk across the Merrimack on the backs of migrating salmon, but the river has come a long way since it was designated one of the 10 dirtiest in the U.S. in 1968. It is to look at, now, and perhaps launch a boat upon. But it is also the reason that all the busy people along its banks are not living and eating Thai food and designing computer graphics systems somewhere else.

# CHAPTER FOUR

# The Connecticut Valley

**Right:** *The name on the barn at this farm near Littleton may be Scottish, but the architecture and red paint both say New England.* CHRISTIAN HEEB

**Facing page:** *Moore Reservoir, viewed from Dodge Hill Recreation Area along the Connecticut near Littleton.* GEORGE WUERTHNER

If the southeastern part of New Hampshire is largely the creation of the mills made possible by the Merrimack River, it is equally true that the western part of the Granite State is testimony to the role played by the Connecticut River as a highway of exploration, settlement and commerce. The resulting landscape was not so much industrial as agricultural. The Connecticut River Valley was populated by farmers from down-country, and the alluvial soil they found was and is the most fertile in New Hampshire.

The westernmost towns of New Hampshire have a good deal in common with the hill-farm communities along the Vermont side of the valley. So similar are their origins, in fact, that many of the towns along the eastern shore nearly became part of Vermont. Settlements on both sides of the river came into being during Governor Benning Wentworth's self-aggrandizing spree of township-chartering, which is why much of pre-revolutionary Vermont was known as the "New Hampshire Grants." New York, in those days, claimed that its jurisdiction reached east to the Connecticut; New Hampshire had decidedly different ideas. For the settlers' part, neither provincial master was worth serving. When, in 1781, Vermont first sought admission to the Union, its territorial claims extended west into New York and east across the Connecticut. This was fine with the New Hampshire towns involved, which had long felt more kinship with the Green Mountain Boys than with the nabobs of Portsmouth. There was even talk of separate treaty terms between Vermont and Great Britain. The border dispute was settled in favor of the present arrangement—with the river as boundary—upon the strong suggestion of the Continental Army's commander-in chief, George Washington. As for any accommodation between England and an independent "Republic of Vermont," there has long been speculation that Washington would have followed up his victory at Yorktown with an expedition into the fractious Green Mountain State.

It has been argued that a separate state straddling the Connecticut might not have been a bad idea—that political divisions work best when they are congruent with social realities. But along the northern Connecticut Valley, this brand of logic was not to prevail. The yeomen of the west bank send their representatives to Montpelier. Across the river, the license plates read "Live Free or Die."

## Littleton

The source of the Connecticut River lies at the northern tip of New Hampshire, in the streams that feed the Connecticut Lakes. But in their uppermost reaches the lands along the river seem more a part of the North Country and the foothills of the White Mountains. The real character of the Connecticut River Valley begins to assert itself from Littleton south.

Although Littleton's western precincts have considerable frontage on the Connecticut, the actual city is built on a smaller, wilder tributary river, the Ammonoosuc. The Ammonoosuc drops a total of 235' through a series of rapids in Littleton; as you walk along Main Street of an evening after the traffic has subsided, the murmur of the

**Above, right to left:** *Otter.* TED LEVIN

*A quiet day in Charleston. Tranquility once came at a premium in this village, settled by Massachusetts pioneers in 1740 as "Number 4" and for a long time the northernmost white outpost in New Hampshire. In 1747, it was the scene of the last attack by the French within the province.* GEORGE WUERTHNER

*Autumn is yard-sale season, here at Keene and everywhere else in New Hampshire.* GEORGE WUERTHNER

**Facing page:** *The Connecticut Valley still is a stronghold of dairying, although the number of individual farms is down and many smaller operators have been squeezed out.* CLYDE H. SMITH

river behind the old brick blocks of commercial buildings is a constant reminder of why the city is here. The earliest harnessing of water power on the Ammonoosuc at Littleton was in 1799, and since then the town has been involved in manufactures as varied as whiskey, carriages, woolen goods, gloves and woodenware. Littleton's most famous products a century ago were hand-held stereoscopes and their double-image cards, with the Kilburn Company of Littleton the *world's* largest manufacturer of them.

Littleton today still makes things—things like shoes and abrasives, and a new black fly bite treatment appropriate to these climes come late spring—but the town's biggest industry is taking care of tourists, particularly skiers, drawn to the nearby White Mountains. A walk down Main Street reveals something of that quality faraway Portsmouth has, of a place at once un-self-consciously workaday yet given to the lightsome

influences of gentrification. A Victorian brick structure inscribed with the words "Tilton's Opera Block 1881" houses, on its ground floor, a combination drugstore/newsstand/soda fountain that appears not to have changed since 1920; alongside is a place called "Not Just Desserts" that advertises itself as a *patisserie.* The only way you would have seen a *patisserie* in a place like Littleton 25 years ago was if some emigrant from Quebec was using his native tongue—and even then, he'd be more likely to open a *boulangerie* and sell white bread. There's a Masonic temple a few doors down from an organic ice cream parlor, and an old-fashioned movie theater across the street from a fitness salon. (The theater, by the way, was the site of the 1941 premiere of "The Great Lie," starring Littleton summer-person Bette Davis.) Anchoring the south side of Main Street are the white-columned Thayers Inn, in continuous operation since 1843, and the venerable

Littleton Diner, cosmetically remodeled on the outside but every bit the 1940s beanery inside. Early on a November morning in the diner, as deer hunters in laced-bottom plaid pants shoveled away eggs and baked beans and a truck driver sat talking with a stringy-haired biker at the counter, I decided that the America of organic ice cream and Nautilus machines had not yet won all the battles in Littleton. A pair of locals in the booth next to mine were having the most ungentrified conversation I have ever heard, rambling from how welfare and state housing assistance were to pay the security deposit on the one fellow's apartment, to the subtleties of romance ("I seen her with another guy." "Yeah, but she still loves me.") to a story of a couple in an apartment on the other side of town who got drunk, started cooking hot dogs, and promptly fell asleep:

"They told the firemen they didn't even know they had hot dogs on the stove."

"Did they get in trouble?

"Oh, yeah. They got thrown out."

This likely will never happen to the guy who just moved, since he probably doesn't cook. Talking about the fine points of his new apartment, he commented that "at least I'll be close to the diner." There you have a certain neighborhood closeness, a community familiarity. I doubt that anyone in Littleton is extolling their new apartment in terms of its nearness to the *patisserie*.

## Farming and the Valley

When you head west toward the Connecticut on Route 135, the region ahead, alongside and to the south of the New England Power Company's Moore Dam and the meandering lake it makes out of this stretch of the Connecticut, offers the first glimpse of the valley's agricultural traditions. They are old traditions, to be sure—I passed a barn in the town of Monroe that bore the date 1790—but they are in greater danger today than at any other time since the migrations to the factory towns and western states in the mid-1800s. To a great extent, agriculture in northern New England means dairying, and dairying is in deep economic trouble. With prices received for milk just barely staying ahead of costs, survival in the

dairy industry involves achieving a certain economy of scale. But most of the New England landscape, including the Connecticut Valley, is incompatible with expansion to the kind of large-acreage enterprises with hundreds of cows typical of New York State's dairy country. New York now supplies between 25 and 30 percent of the milk consumed in the Boston Market, a federally-designated area made up of most of New England excluding Maine and parts of New Hampshire and Vermont. New Hampshire's contribution towards slaking the market's 620-million-gallon thirst was only 6.4 percent, or approximately 40 million gallons. Another, starker set of figures tells the story of what has become of dairying in New Hampshire: in 1976, there were 522 dairy farms in the Granite State. By 1981, the figure was down to 460, and in 1986 there were only 356. The surviving farmers are getting more milk per cow, from more cows, on farms with a higher average acreage—but throughout the state, and in the Connecticut Valley, both the number of cows and the number of acres farmed have diminished. If

New Hampshire agriculture is to survive outside of a handful of large, consolidated dairy operations, it will be through diversification and certain lucrative areas of specialization. In the more northerly parts of the Connecticut Valley, Christmas trees are an increasingly popular cash crop.

Other farmers are turning to sheep, goats and relatively "exotic" cattle breeds such as the Simmental. (I passed one farm in the upper valley that raises Shetland ponies.) Some make specialty cheeses; others concentrate on vegetable growing for farmstands and city markets, or packaging manure to be used as lawn fertilizer. The self-reliance and adaptability demonstrated by many of New Hampshire's farmers is encouraging, but there can be no doubt that the Currier and Ives vision of the "golden age," and the integrity of rural communities of which it spoke, is never to return to the valley of the Connecticut.

## Covered Bridges—And Upper Valley Towns

Woodsville, technically a part of Bath Township, is an old railroad center located at the point

where the Ammonoosuc flows into the Connecticut River. Here the tracks of the Boston & Maine met those of the Canadian Pacific. Woodsville's location athwart these two lines made the little sawmill town into an important regional rail capital; so strong is the local identification with the iron horse that the high school athletic teams are called the "Engineers." But as you drive into Woodsville from the north on Route 135, you'll cross the Ammonoosuc on a transportation fixture that predates the coming of the railroad to these parts by more than a quarter of a century. This is the 1827 Haverhill-Bath covered bridge, one of three in the town of Bath. It is by no means large by New Hampshire standards—another of Bath's covered bridges, built in 1832, measures 400′ in length. The town's citizens recently voted by a narrow margin to restore that bridge, right down to its great, arching wooden trusses. The cost was roughly $600 per resident, but a properly-cared-for covered bridge probably will stand another 150 years. Come hell or high water, we're tempted to say, but we can't be sure about the latter.

Why were bridges covered in the first place? There are almost as many answers as there are country sages to offer them—including the suggestion that horses were less likely to become skittish in mid-crossing if they couldn't look down at the water. The reason that seems most plausible, however, is that the builders simply wanted to protect the wooden structure from the elements.

Just south of Woodsville, on Route 10, is a marker that darkly reminds us of conditions in the upper valley before the bridges were built and the hill farms settled, when this was the dangerous fringe of New England. Here, at a point two miles below the confluence of the Ammonoosuc and the Connecticut, the colonial guerrilla leader Robert Rogers and his famed "Rogers' Rangers" planned to rendezvous with a supply party after destroying the Indian village of St. Francis, Quebec on October 4, 1759. The men were near exhaustion, and their food had run out. But the French and Indian casualties at St. Francis were avenged when the Rangers discovered that their relief party had come and gone. Many of them died of starvation and exposure. As the marker

grimly puts it, "early settlers found their bones along these intervales."

The intervales that lie among the hills between Woodsville and Hanover today are among the prettiest parts of the Connecticut Valley, and of all New Hampshire. The landscape alternates between snug little towns and empty valleys, once farmed but now grown back to forest, that seem like the loneliest places in New England outside the great Maine woods. But the next town always comes along quickly enough, just when you crest a hill and expect another stretch of forest. The surprise in Haverhill is its large, neat common, bordered on one side by the

*Above:* The Bath-Swiftwater covered bridge spans the Ammonoosuc River at Swiftwater, near Woodsville. Barely visible is the enormous wooden arch that supports the ancient structure. JEFF GNASS

*Facing page:* Governor Benning Wentworth granted Colonel Benjamin Bellows the charter for the valley town of Walpole (seen here) in 1752. The colonel's name is preserved today in the small Vermont city across the river, Bellows Falls. NONA BAUER

*Above:* The Connecticut River separates Orford, New Hampshire (right) from Fairlee, Vermont. Washington Irving called Orford the most beautiful town he'd seen. CLYDE H. SMITH

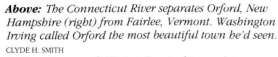

*Right:* Dartmouth Winter Carnival ice sculpture: "The Starshooter," 1940 (DARTMOUTH COLLEGE ARCHIVES)

*Facing page, top:* The campus of Dartmouth College in Hanover. HANSON CARROLL

*Bottom:* The Dartmouth College Green, a campus beyond time. Is it 1958, or 1988? All we know is that it isn't 1968. CHRISTIAN HEEB

brick buildings of Haverhill Academy, now a junior high school. Had Eleazer Wheelock accepted the town's offer of 50 acres in 1770, a much larger institution would have surrounded the Haverhill Common today. But Wheelock turned Haverhill down, and instead built his Dartmouth College farther south in Hanover. Haverhill was left to be remembered as the home of Colonel Charles Johnston, a hero of the Battle of Bennington (his c. 1770 house stands near the common), and as the site, in the 1860s, of the last public hanging in New Hampshire.

Orford is the loveliest of all the upper valley towns—and, in the opinion of no less traveled a writer than Washington Irving, the most beautiful he had seen in the United States or Europe. The town's outstanding architectural feature is the string of seven mansions, built between 1773 and 1839, that line "The Ridge" above Route 10 and

the river. One, the c. 1815 General John B. Wheeler House at the southern end of the row, was designed by Asher Benjamin during his association with Charles Bulfinch. It's easy to imagine that living in one of these Orford mansions, and looking down just after dawn to see the mist rise over the Connecticut, must have been one of the most pleasant experiences 19th-century upper-class rural American life could have afforded. For most of us today, the next best thing will have to be a night spent in one of the upper valley's gracious inns. There is a good one on the common at Lyme, where you can rest up for a day at Hanover and the campus of Dartmouth College.

## Vox Clamantis In Deserto

The Latin motto of Dartmouth—translated as "A Voice Crying in the Wilderness"—is no longer appropriate to this Ivy League school, in terms

either of its physical remoteness or of its visibility on the national scene. But there was a very sound reason for applying the biblical quote to the college when it was founded, in 1770, on the frontiers of colonial New Hampshire.

Look carefully at the official seal the Dartmouth motto adorns and you'll see American Indians gathering at a single school building in the forest. This is no allegorical representation, but a visual description of the actual circumstances of the school's founding. Dartmouth was the brainchild of Reverend Eleazer Wheelock of Lebanon, Connecticut, who had been teaching and Christianizing young Indians in his home since the 1740s. During the 1760s, he began soliciting money for a full-scale Indian school (one of his most successful fund raisers was his first student, the Mohegan Samson Occom for whom Hanover's Occom Pond is named), and he received his charter in 1769. The new institution was named after the Earl of Dartmouth, an early backer of the plan.

Just as the seal shows, Dartmouth did start out in a lone building on the edge of the woods, and its library began with a box containing knives, forks and books that Reverend Wheelock carted north to the five-year-old settlement of Hanover. There were Indians among the first group of young men to take instruction at Dartmouth, but they never arrived in any significant numbers; soon the new college was a white man's institution. The first graduating class, in 1771, numbered four; 20 years later, 49 men took their degrees from Dartmouth.

The greatest event of Dartmouth's early years might have been of importance only in the context of the college's history, had it not involved Dartmouth's most famous alumnus and the establishment of a vital precedent concerning the inviolability of contracts under United States law. This was the Dartmouth College Case, precipitated in 1816 when the New Hampshire legislature attempted to alter the 1769 charter and create a state-controlled "Dartmouth University" around the older, heretofore-independent entity. The trustees and most of the students balked, with the latter meeting privately for classes. Eventually, the

after its short troublesome span has been forgotten, students of the law and friends of Dartmouth College remember the close of Webster's argument before Marshall:

"Sir, you may destroy this little institution; it is weak, it is in your hands! I know it is one of the lesser lights in the literary horizon of our country. You may put it out; but if you do, you must carry through your work! You must extinguish, one after another, all those great lights of science which, for more than a century, have thrown their radiance over the land! It is, sir, as I have said, a small college, but yet there are those who love it!"

And so Dartmouth was free to grow and prosper as an independent college, which it has. The early 20th century was a particularly vigorous era of expansion, during which the college not only acquired its Ivy League patina but achieved the front-rank academic status that it continues to enjoy today. (A recent polling of American college and university presidents placed it among the top 15 institutions of higher learning in the country.) Of the traditions Dartmouth initiated during this era, perhaps the one most familiar to the public is the Winter Carnival. Since 1911, the annual February event has drawn students and outsiders alike to its ice sculptures, nonstop parties and sporting events including competition on Hanover's own 30-meter ski jump. Outdoor sports, competitive or otherwise, long have been a Dartmouth mainstay. The Dartmouth Outing Club takes tremendous advantage of the school's natural setting, with programs in skiing, hiking, climbing, canoeing and myriad other aspects of what Ivy Leaguer Teddy Roosevelt (Harvard, not Dartmouth) called the "strenuous life." All beginning freshmen are asked to join faculty and staff on a long hiking trip through the White Mountains.

Academically, Dartmouth remains strong in mathematics, English, romance languages, history, chemistry, and geology. Computer science is given special attention. The computer language BASIC was developed here by former Dartmouth president John Kemeny. Since 1985, each dormitory room has been equipped with a terminal connected to the college's central computer. And

trustees sued to have the 1816 contract revision reversed, and the "University" with its gubernatorially-appointed overseers abolished. With financial help from General John Wheeler (he of the Orford mansion), they got their case to the U.S. Supreme Court; Daniel Webster, Dartmouth 1801, served as counsel.

Daniel Webster was 36 years old in 1818. He had been born on a farm in Salisbury, New Hampshire in 1782, the son of a Revolutionary War veteran. (His birthplace still stands, off Route 127 a couple of miles west of Franklin.) Having been educated at Philips Exeter and Dartmouth, he completed his legal studies in Boston. His first law office was in Boscawen, New Hampshire; later he spent nine years practicing in Portsmouth, where he became involved in Federalist politics. He was elected to two terms in Congress before moving to Massachusetts, the state in which he

lived during his years of triumph as congressman, senator and United States secretary of state. Yet Webster always kept a home in New Hampshire, and the state reveres him still as its greatest native son. Dartmouth harbors the same proprietary feelings about the man who, when he pleaded its case before the Supreme Court, was yet to become the "godlike Daniel" of American legend. He was our greatest orator, one of our finest legal intellects, a commanding human presence on a par with Washington and Lincoln…and the only one in our national mythology ever to have bested the Devil in debate.

When the Dartmouth College Case was heard in the Supreme Court, Webster prevailed before Chief Justice John Marshall and his associates, thus helping to establish the right of federal protection for state-chartered institutions. "Dartmouth University" was no more—but today, long

the Dartmouth Medical School has become a full-fledged medical center, serving the Connecticut Valley through two hospitals and a number of smaller clinics as well as providing medical training.

Dartmouth and Hanover have become virtually synonymous. The center of both the college and the town is the lovely College Green. Along the eastern side of the Green rise the austere white facades of Wentworth and Dartmouth halls, the latter a replica of a 1791 college building that stood on this site until it burned in 1904. The structure facing the Green from the south fits in so well it could easily be a college administration building, but this stately neo-Georgian pile is actually the posh Hanover Inn. It's an 18th-century set-piece down to the furniture, which is more reminiscent of colonial Portsmouth than the wilderness Eleazer Wheelock cried out in. Just around the corner from the inn, South Main Street forms the axis of a commercial district that would make you realize this was a college town even if you'd come in blindfolded and hadn't seen the college. Five movie theaters, 17 clothing shops, and nearly two dozen restaurants are not the common run of things in New England villages of 7,000 souls. Hanover is a small town, yet there are those who love its patés and imported ales.

### The Cornish Colony

South of the nuts-and-bolts commercial strip in Lebanon that serves as a foil to Hanover's upscale shops, the Connecticut Valley regains its bucolic character. The rolling hills and occasional open vistas along this stretch of the river were a great attraction to the members of the informal "Cornish Colony" who summered in and around the town of Cornish between the years 1885 and 1935. The first, and most famous, of their number was the sculptor Augustus Saint-Gaudens. Saint-Gaudens' home, "Aspet," is maintained by the federal government as a national historic site. Here are the studios, gardens and grave site of the man who sculpted the famous "Standing Lincoln" and Boston's Robert Gould Shaw Memorial; a gallery exhibits copies of several of his other works,

notably the striding "Puritan." Saint-Gaudens spent summers here until 1897, and lived at Aspet year-round from 1900 until his death in 1907.

Among the prominent figures in the arts who joined Saint-Gaudens in Cornish around the turn of the century, and continued to be associated

*Above:* Augustus Saint-Gaudens' "Little Studio" at his Cornish estate, now a National Historic Site. The bronze sculptures are "Diana" and "Lincoln the Man."

*Facing page:* The Connecticut River Valley near Piermont. HANSON CARROLL

**Above:** *Monroe, on the Connecticut River.*
**Right:** *Canada goose.* HANSON CARROLL PHOTOS

with the area after his death, were the poet Percy MacKaye; the dramatists Langdon Mitchell, Philip Littell and Louis Evans Shipman; sculptor Herbert Adams; and the architect Charles A. Platt. Novelist Winston Churchill, known in New Hampshire for his progressive candidacy for the governorship as well as for his books, was also a devotee of Cornish's hills and valleys. His house, which burned in 1923, was used for three years as a summer retreat by President Woodrow Wilson. But it was a painter named Stephen Parrish whose summer residence here led to the longest-standing relationship between any artist and the region. His son was Maxfield Parrish, the preeminent American illustrator of the early 20th century and a theme painter of no small accomplishment. The younger Parrish spent much of his long life (1870-1966) in Plainfield, just north of Cornish, at a big house that he built in 1898 and filled with family and friends. The rambling Parrish house was severely damaged by fire in the early 1980s; following its renovation and sale to a private owner, the Parrish canvases once housed in an adjacent museum were sold. But even if we can no longer go to Plainfield to see a collection of Maxfield Parrish's work, it is possible to enjoy the same valley scenes he captured so faithfully in paintings like "New Hampshire" and "Afterglow"—and if we're lucky, the evening sky will turn to that electrically-charged hue known today as "Parrish blue."

We can't leave the subject of Cornish without mentioning that it is the home of the American literary figure least likely to be part of a "colony," coterie or chowder society of any kind. This is the novelist and short-story writer J.D. Salinger, whose celebrated penchant for absolute privacy has brought any number of would-be interviewers and garden-variety intruders to this corner of New Hampshire. I do not count myself among them, but I will confess to turning off Route 12A, the river road, to see what sort of town a man so bent on seclusion might pick to live in. I can report that Salinger has chosen the right place for throwing his pursuers off track. Within five minutes I had no idea whether I was in Cornish Mills, Cornish City, Cornish Center or Cornish Flat.

I'd have stopped for directions back to 12A, but was deathly afraid of picking Salinger's house by sheer happenstance and being felled by a withering stare or worse.

## The Lower Valley and Some Latter-Day Settlers

Claremont is a small city, just south of Cornish, with an economy precariously based on the survival of its paper and machine-tool industries. It is the only sizeable city (approximately 15,000) of New Hampshire's lower Connecticut Valley. The drill bits that opened the gold fields of the South African Transvaal were developed in Claremont; today, as in its sister city of Springfield, Vermont across the river, the surviving machine shops depend upon adaptability to specialty manufactures to stay in business. Perhaps they will, although a more likely scenario would see Claremont become an extension of the high-tech axis that is extending from Nashua through Peterborough and Keene, which is also the home of Keene State College and thus the southwestern cornerstone of the state university system. Time will tell.

Over the past 20 years the valley has also attracted "industries" that fit under neither the high-tech nor heavy manufacturing label. These are the home- and shop-based crafts operations initiated by individuals who are often newcomers to the area, to the state, or even to New England itself. John and Debbie Mahan are New Jersey natives who came to the town of Walpole in 1980, after living for several years in Vermont. They are jewelers, working in silver. Neither had any notion of becoming an artisan when the couple lived in and around Jersey City; as John Mahan recalls, "in New Jersey, we never knew that you could not only make silver jewelry but actually make a living at it. Everybody we knew worked regular jobs. When we got here, things seemed freer—I don't know why, but you can do things like that. Everyone I met here had his or her own business—weaving, woodworking, running little restaurants—so we figured we might as well give it a shot too. I had a feeling that this would be a good place to learn a skill."

The Mahans are in their late 30s now. They arrived in Vermont in the early 1970s, when the cities of the East Coast were sending rural New England college-educated veterans of a quick tour of duty with the counterculture, who were determined to do anything but sit at a desk. A lot of them are sitting at desks now, in Burlington and Manchester and Portland, but the ones who became good artisans—and the Mahans are very good jewelers—have succeeded in their escape. Find a country craftsman around the age of 40 who isn't a native of upcountry New England, and

**Top:** *Streamline Moderne in the Connecticut Valley. a diner interior at Claremont.* CHRISTIAN HEEB

**Left:** *Win Tri-State Megabucks, and you'll never want for night crawlers again: a general store in Monroe.* GEORGE WUERTHNER

**Right:** *A farmstand near Wilton.* GEORGE WUERTHNER

*Above:* A large Connecticut Valley dairy farm, evidence of the economies of scale. The days of the hillfarm with two dozen cows are over.
*Facing page:* Downtown Keene at Christmas.

chances are you've found the product of some English department located within 30 miles of Times or Harvard Square.

John Mahan and I talked in his Walpole workshop one day, while he worked on a lost-wax casting for a silver pendant. John is a man of medium build with thinning black hair and a big black mustache; he wears denim jeans with nobody's name on the pocket and a blue chambray shirt. I asked him if there had been a support system up here, perhaps something like an apprenticeship arrangement that might help an emigré from New Jersey to get started as an artisan. "No," he told me. "There weren't any apprentice positions in the strict sense of the word. But a support system? It was excellent—there was a sense of camaraderie, of encouragement from the people you met. Most of them were self-taught, too, and we all understood each other."

Does that kind of community feeling still exist in the valley? Could John and Debbie Mahan have come here in the late 1980s, learned a skill, and done well with it? "It wouldn't be as easy," John surmises. "First of all, you'd probably be by yourself. The generation gap has flipped over; young people aren't doing this sort of thing. Even if they were, it's harder to buy or rent here now. The lower valley is getting to be a bedroom suburb for people who work in Keene, and some even live here weekends and work in Boston all week. Land values are way up." A wry Jersey edge comes into Mahan's voice. "It's hard to be a hippie now."

## South to Monadnock

You can follow Route 12 down along the Connecticut River from Claremont and east to Keene, and get a fair idea of what John Mahan meant by these towns becoming bedroom communities. They aren't suburbs, by any means, but there's no denying the farms have begun to thin out. But a more meandering route from Claremont to Keene will take you through some of the loneliest little hill towns of southern New Hampshire, places that look as if no one in them ever gave a thought to commuting to Boston. The back roads of Unity and Lempster make even Cornish seem logical; when you finally arrive in Lempster itself, you have arrived at an ancient grange hall, a combination post office and one-pump gas station with the oldest Gulf sign in the world, and a handful of houses. Rod Serling will be by soon to tell you it is 1936. On a gray November afternoon, Lempster is the very end of the earth.

Other hill towns, though infinitesimal and far off the beaten track, boast a single impressive structure. Trim little Acworth comes to a crest at its United Church, a Palladian jewel built in 1821. In Alstead, an exquisite granite Beaux Arts temple turns out to be the town library, donated in 1910

by a local boy who got rich in Chicago. But nowhere do the buildings in the towns speak as eloquently of the past as the low stone walls in the woods. These were the walls that once marked pastures during that "golden age" when farming was the business of New Hampshire.

Whatever roads you take through southwestern New Hampshire, they should lead to Jaffrey and Mt. Monadnock. A mere slip of a mountain compared to the lofty peaks of the Presidential Range, 3,165′ Monadnock is nevertheless a New Hampshire icon. It rises gently but majestically from the forest that surrounds it, and offers a clear-day prospect of sights as distant as the Boston skyline and Mt. Washington itself, more than 100 miles away. Its trails invite even the casual hiker to its summit, conveniently treeless for 360° views. (There were trees here once, but settlers burned

them nearly 200 years ago to rout wolves. The summit rock was scoured clean of soil, leaving the mountain as we see it today.) Even if you don't care to ascend Monadnock, you can enjoy it from countless points in the surrounding valleys. Unlike many larger peaks, it isn't crowded from view by its neighbors.

That is because it hasn't any neighbors. The very word "monadnock," taken from the Abnaki name for this mountain, refers to any erosion-resistant mountain or mass of rock that stands isolated in a plain. This is the original of the type, in man's understanding if not in actual geological age. Unperturbed by time and glaciers, it appeals to the Yankee mind as a symbol of stoic independence. It has the command of a simple fact, and the respect of people who live below it in the towns of the lower Connecticut Valley.

# CHAPTER FIVE

# Central New Hampshire & The Lakes Region

***Right:*** *Meredith, on the western shore of Lake Winnipesaukee, calls itself the "Latchkey to the White Mountains." The Loon Preservation Committee is headquartered here.*
© GARY BRAASCH

***Facing page:*** *A general store in Danbury. No, that isn't an antique "Moxie" sign; people in New England still drink Moxie.* TOM BEAN

Of all the fictional portrayals of New Hampshire and New Hampshire life—from Kenneth Roberts' *Northwest Passage* to Thornton Wilder's *Our Town* to the Hollywood-meets-Dartmouth movie *Winter Carnival*—perhaps the images most vivid in the American mind during the decade of the 1980s are from a film set in the Granite State's central lakes region. This was *On Golden Pond*, in which Henry Fonda's crusty retired professor

Norman Thayer comes to grips with his daughter and step-grandson during a summer spent at his lakeside camp. Not that the film made much ado about being set in New Hampshire. From the looks of the house, the landscape and the old speedboat, it could just as easily have taken place in the Adirondacks. But there was a New Hampshire *feel* about *On Golden Pond*, and it didn't only have to do with Norman Thayer's

Yankee irascibility. New Hampshire is where the film was shot. There is indeed a "Golden Pond," and its real name is Squam Lake.

Squam wanders across the map just to the northwest of Winnipesaukee, in the heart of New Hampshire's lakes region. This state was dealt most of its water in one concentrated, central area, and Squam is the second-largest of its more than 1,300 glacially-gouged lakes and ponds. But for all its size, and the archetypal summer-at-the-lake character it conveys in *On Golden Pond,* Squam isn't entirely representative of New Hampshire's inland waters. It is as beautiful as any of them, no doubt about it. And it is popular in the summer. The difference lies in the type of popularity it enjoys: Squam may have the most generic name of any lake in New Hampshire (it's an abridgement of an Indian word for water, *asquam),* but it has about as much in common with the louder precincts of Winnipesaukee's shore as loons have with starlings. With the exception of one stretch of the back road that connects Center Sandwich with Center Harbor, hardly any of the routes that encircle Squam Lake come anywhere near its shores. The only commercial establishments are a couple of stores and a marina, clustered on Route 3 at the narrow channel connecting Squam and Little Squam lakes. There are no condominiums in sight. The cottages on Squam Lake are all built a certain distance from the shore, per regulations set down by the Squam Lake Association, and all are painted in subtle colors that don't clash with the forest. You can't see the houses from the main roads around the lake; the only signs of their presence are the narrow gravel drives that lead toward the water. They are discreet summer houses that belong to discreet people, many of whom pass them down from generation to generation. One gets the feeling that many of the folks who live down those narrow drives would be comfortable at tea with Professor and Mrs. Thayer…and one understands why they were less than thrilled when the film put their big little lake on the map. No doubt there is an occasional Fondaesque harrumph at mention of the local innkeeper who runs tours of the lake pointing out *On Golden Pond* sites, such as the rocks where

*Above: A 19th century image of Squam Lake, looking somewhat more heavily peppered with islands than it does in real life.* COURTESY NEW HAMPSHIRE HISTORICAL SOCIETY
*Right: The* Mount Washington *is the last of the big excursion boats on Lake Winnipesaukee. Its namesake predecessor steamed back and forth across the lake for 67 years, from 1872 to 1939.* CLYDE H. SMITH

*Facing page: Squam Lake in summer. Local residents' self-policing has kept development impact minimal along the shoreline; from the water, the surrounding terrain looks more like wilderness than it really is* CLYDE H. SMITH

Norman and the kid wrecked that beautiful mahogany runabout.

## Different Lakes, Different Styles

For better or worse, we have to head to the other big lakes such as Winnipesaukee and Newfound to capture the character of the lakes region today. *Golden Pond*-style subtlety has not always been the signature characteristic of development in New Hampshire's freshwater playground. Perhaps a certain tone was set by the second Governor John Wentworth, who chose a site on Lake Wentworth as the site of his summer estate. The governor started building a mansion 100′ long, with six-foot windows and a 12′-wide central hallway, which would rival any of the

Georgian palaces in Portsmouth. He began summering there in 1770, although the place still wasn't finished by the time the Revolution precipitated his move to Nova Scotia. Wentworth's property was connected with Portsmouth via a 45-mile road he had built, and which he extended to Hanover in 1771 so that he could attend the first commencement exercises at Dartmouth. His wife hated the trip between the seacoast and the lake— "I dread the journey, as the roads are so bad," she once confided in a letter—but the governor's bumpy carriage trail did help open the lakes region to settlement, and gave Wolfeboro the right to call itself "the oldest summer resort in America." That's one of those unprovable but harmless sobriquets that no one ever seeks to challenge.

The lakes didn't immediately spring to life as a landlocked Jersey shore. Walking the west shore of Winnipesaukee in the summer of 1841, the 18-year-old future historian Francis Parkman found little more than log cabins along Alton Bay and the southern part of the lake, and farms farther north. He wasn't pleased with the land clearing that had been done to accommodate the latter, and wrote in his diary that the absence of trees "lay the road open to the baking sun." During the second half of the 19th century, though, a number of the finer lakeside farms became the estates of wealthy "summer people" from the cities of New England, while the arrival of the railroad at places like Wolfeboro, Alton Bay, Weirs Beach and Meredith made possible the democratization of summer vacationing as represented by the proliferation of hotels and seasonal boarding houses. One phenomenon of the railroad era was the coming of large passenger steamboats to Lake Winnipesaukee. The Concord and Montreal Railroad launched its *Lady of the Lake* in 1849. It was followed by steamers such as the *Seneca* and the *Maid of the Isles*, the *Ossipee* and the Boston and Maine (B&M) Railroad's *Chocorua*. (The *Chocorua* did double duty as a hotel for camp-meeting attendants while she was moored at Alton Bay.) The most famous and best-loved of all Winnipesaukee excursion boats was the *Mount Washington*, launched by the B&M in 1872 at Alton Bay. It survived until 1939, by which time it was believed to be the oldest boat running on American inland waters. Its successor, also named *Mount Washington*, still plies the routes between Winnipesaukee ports today. Another sign of the lake's popularity with summer visitors was the 1903 inauguration of rural free delivery via mail boat, a tradition that continues today with the *Sophie C's* June-to-September mail runs. The *Sophie C* carries excursion passengers, and offers a unique opportunity for visitors to the lake to get a close look at some of its 274 habitable isles. Some patrons of the lake boats have more than a casual cruise in mind. On a bright October day in 1987, I stopped at the little restored depot in Weirs Beach, used as a station for the seasonal Winnipesaukee Railroad and as a dock and ticket office for the *Mount Washington*,

*Sophie C* and *Doris E.* While I was waiting for the *Mount Washington* to heave into view from behind a nearby island, a party of eight to 10 people around the age of 50, wearing suits and dresses, arrived at the dock with flowers, cameras and a big cake box. The man and woman around whom this little party seemed to center were both wearing derbies. Of course they were there to get married on the *Mount Washington;* as the groom put it, "we're the entertainment for the day." The big boat showed up on time, scheduled for one of its last trips of the season. The minister said he was glad he'd brought his sweater.

Occasional chill breezes notwithstanding, golden autumn days like the one the wedding party enjoyed well may be the best time for visiting Winnipesaukee, Newfound or the other large New Hampshire lakes. The simple fact is that in the century and a half since Francis Parkman took his hot and lonesome walk, the lakes—especially the west shore of Winnipesaukee—have become a little too popular for their own good. Although there are still some lovely, unspoiled stretches along the shore (the scenic drive through Ellacoya State Beach on Route 11 is especially fine), more and more of the land adjacent to the lakes has become prime development property that is especially busy in the summer. And although traffic dies down after Labor Day, buildings are no respecter of seasons.

73

"Scenic Heights Condo's" *(sic)* reads a sign just outside the state property at Ellacoya. There are condos everywhere: tasteful, tacky, luxurious, spartan, you name it. On Route 3A along the east side of Newfound Lake, there are old hotels that have been converted to condos, along with a scattering of 1950s motels and tourist courts that may go the same route. Newfound, located above Bristol east of the Pemigewasset River and Interstate 93, presents a particular set of development problems. It is a big, open lake, without a convoluted shoreline and myriad islands like Winnipesaukee. Consequently its shoreline has largely become a "houseline" of freestanding cottages and cluster developments. What few islands there are on Newfound are developed. Rounding the north shore of the lake on the way to Hebron, I did a double take upon seeing an islet no bigger than the house that stood on it. I had to wonder about the sewage arrangements: this isn't Venice, and there is no tide. The new construction is even creeping up the slopes north of the lake. As a hitchhiking Hebron native told me, "nowadays there's a neighbor everywhere you look." Clearly, the local conservation commissions beginning to gain power in the lakes region face some hard thinking about how to shape growth, and how to decide when an area has reached its carrying capacity. The gingerbread Victorian cottages at funky old Weirs Beach were the beginning of a vacation-home boom whose end we haven't seen yet.

Along with the summer homes come the boats. As one Meredith resident put it, "On a summer weekend, you can almost walk across Lake Winnipesaukee on the boats." No one wants to tell people that they can't buy or own boats—least of all in live-free-or-die New Hampshire—but the state has recently addressed the task of controlling the Winnipesaukee armada by imposing a moratorium on new moorings. This approach has been only partially effective, since there are plenty of dry dock facilities in the lakes region. People just put their boats in the water in the morning, and take them out at night.

## The Living Symbols of the Lakes

The proliferation of boats and buildings spawned by central New Hampshire's recreational boom often has worked to the disadvantage of one of the region's oldest and most truly representative inhabitants—the common loon.

The loon is one of nature's emblems, a living signpost that tells you where you are in the world. Some birds—the mallard duck, for instance—are true cosmopolitans, at home in so many places that they can never be identified with a specific location. But the loon carries with it a spirit of place, and that place is the lake country of the northern United States and Canada. The harrowing cry and idiot laugh of the loon still are common enough north of the border, but over much of its New England range the bird's population long since has been reduced to minuscule numbers. Loons are sensitive creatures that do not easily suffer fools, miscreants or even innocent trespassers: as humans have advanced across the New England landscape, the loons have retreated. This has been especially true over the course of the last century's development of New Hampshire lakefront. From late spring until fall, loons occupy specific ecological niches on northern lakes, on undisturbed islands and stretches of shoreline.

*Above: A nesting loon. The "Great Northern Diver," as it is sometimes called, has evolved a form more at home in water than on land or in the air. **Left:** having recorded the dimensions of this adult loon, a Loon Preservation Committee worker prepares to release the bird.* TED LEVIN PHOTOS

***Facing page, top:*** *The march of condominiums: an as-yet-to-be-landscaped scene near Laconia, at the southern end of Lake Winnipesaukee.* GEORGE WUERTHNER ***Bottom left:*** *An equestrian event at Sandwich. Look for stock-car racing in other parts of the state; here in the northern lakes district, the residents set a different tone.* CLYDE H. SMITH ***Right:*** *Yes, it's a camera. Is that a sailboat? The place is Spofford Lake.* GEORGE WUERTHNER

(They migrate in winter to coastal points from Massachusetts south.) Their most important requirement, aside from access to a steady diet of fish, is to be left unmolested during nesting and while rearing their chicks before fall migration. They are a barometer of an area's wildness; they can't get along with hordes of people. But destruction of habitat and outright harassment, as in some unfortunate incidents involving motorboats, are only part of the problem. The natural predators of loon eggs, such as gulls and raccoons, coexist very nicely with human beings in a symbiosis based on garbage. Most loon chicks that die are lost in the egg stage; once they hatch, the survival rate is 80 to 90 percent.

In Meredith, at the westernmost corner of Lake Winnipesaukee, a remarkable organization called the Loon Preservation Committee (LPC) has led the battle to reverse loon population declines in all New England. An outgrowth of the New Hampshire Audubon Society and an affiliate of the North American Loon Fund, the LPC has worked since 1976 at the twin tasks of monitoring the nest-

ing birds and waging a vigorous public education program to minimize impact of human encounters. It does this with a full-time office staff of three, eight summer field workers—and a volunteer team of more than 3,000 "cooperators" watching every lake or pond in New England that has a breeding pair of loons. If loons rode the subways, these people would be the Guardian Angels.

I stopped in the little lakeside city of Meredith one day to talk with Betsy McCoy, a Maryland native serving as acting director of the Loon Preservation Committee. McCoy is a 1986 graduate of University of New Hampshire's Wildlife Management Program, and a veteran of two summers' field work with the LPC. At 23, she projected a good deal more confidence about her career than most people 10 years her senior, and her entirely appropriate "power suit" was a pair of corduroys, a sweater and hiking boots. Except for that mature sense of purpose, she might have fit on a college campus of 1970.

"I first took a job with the LPC because it was an opportunity for experience in my field, and not

because of any prior involvement I'd had with this particular species," said McCoy. "For most people, it's the other way around. But now I see that it wouldn't be hard to fill a lifetime with loons."

Much of McCoy's work centers on coordinating the efforts of the LPC's volunteers, who by all accounts are an enthusiastic and dedicated lot.

"People are so fascinated by loons, they start talking about the birds on the lakes where they live as 'their' loons," she told me. "They conduct loon watches; they escort the loons from their nests to their brooding territories with boats; some even donate land for nest sites. If they find someone inadvertently bothering the birds—for instance, fishing too close to a nest—they'll tell them. And the people who have been chased away understand, and often become avid volunteers themselves. Loons bring something out in people. They're a doorway to environmental awareness. A volunteer will get interested in loons, and next he'll become interested in general environmental-quality issues, maybe even serve on a conservation commission. As of summer 1987 we had seventeen nesting pairs of loons on Winnipesaukee. In the early seventies there were probably only four or five. The reason is the folks who become involved."

The loons' recent breeding successes also have been helped by a bit of low-tech ingenuity called the artificial island. Water level is crucial to nesting loons. Despite their well known abilities as swimmers and divers, the birds can do little more than flop helplessly on land. Thus the loons (who mate for life, according to the best evidence) choose nesting sites that are very close to the water, and to which they return year after year. If lake levels rise, the sites are inundated; if levels fall significantly, the birds cannot reach their preferred nesting spots. To increase the odds for successful nesting, the Loon Preservation Committee occasionally uses "artificial islands"—constructions of cedar logs, rotting wood, wire mesh, sod and nesting material. Since the fake islands float, they can compensate for the loss of shoreline or natural island nesting sites when water level variations are acute. Another technique is even simpler: it involves talking with local hydro power

companies, and getting them to keep water levels as steady as possible between mid-May and the end of August, when loons are on their nests. For the most part, the hydro people have been listening—and, says Betsy McCoy, potential developers also are sensitive to the loons' nesting requirements. "They're aware of the public concerns, and are willing to work around them."

Does all this—the number of ready volunteers, the hydro and developers' cooperation—point to a loon mystique? Betsy McCoy thinks so, and cites *On Golden Pond's* footage of loons as being partly responsible for putting the birds in the public eye. Their popularity is certainly borne out by a casual inspection of the shelves at a country store like the one in Moultonborough: here are stuffed toy loons, loon magnets, loon paperweights, loon calendars, loon datebooks…in New Hampshire, at least, loons are the whales of the 1980s. But behind the trappings of faddism is something real, something important. There ought to be loons—there ought to be creatures who can paint a picture of the place where they live with nothing more than the sound of their voices.

***Above:*** *Turk's Head squash, named in a less ethnically sensitive time because of the turban shape. These are a nuisance to peel, but delicious when boiled and pureed with a dash of maple syrup.* ***Left:*** *Apple blossom time.* NONA BAUER PHOTOS

***Facing page:*** *Streeter Pond in autumn.* CLYDE H. SMITH

77

*A homestead at New Hampton, flush with the spirit of the season.* CLYDE H. SMITH

## "Sandwich Home Industries" & Their Legacy

The town of Center Sandwich lies just north and east of Squam Lake. It is one of those stereotypical white-steepled New England villages, neat as a pin and peppered with just the right assortment of old-time and modern country businesses: a general store, an inn, a cabinetmaker, a picture framer, an auction house, a realtor and a place that provides home secretarial services. In the middle of it all is a shop operated by the League of New Hampshire Craftsmen. With its pottery, hand-weavings, jars of jelly and hot pepper relish, and silkscreened cards, it resembles all of the other League stores throughout the state. But Center Sandwich is different. This is where the whole idea got started.

The League of New Hampshire Craftsmen was born out of that same melding of local and out-of-town resources that gives a town like Center Sandwich its present-day character. The "flatlanders," as upcountry New England people sometimes call them, can be a demanding and intrusive force; sometimes neither rural society nor the rural landscape can survive the culture shock that accompanies too large an influx of summer people, especially when they start staying year-round. But when the right individuals are involved, outsiders can be a welcome leaven in a country town. That was the case with Mr. and Mrs. J. Randolph Coolidge, a wealthy Massachusetts couple living in Center Sandwich in the late 1920s.

It was Mrs. Coolidge who first conceived of turning the ancient, inherited handicraft skills of her neighbors into an economic resource for the craftspeople themselves and the town. Having convinced her architect husband of the plan's feasibility and enlisted his support, she decided to focus first on rug hooking. A rug exhibit and talk, using local resources and held in the town library, served as a catalyst to get the people of Sandwich and environs thinking about their own abilities. They were, after all, not many generations removed from the days when nearly all country people were artisans by necessity. The time was right to preserve old skills, as well as for using them for local profit.

Within two years the craftspeople of Sandwich were displaying and selling their wares in a small shop in the village, and an institution called the Sandwich Home Industries was born. The shop and its network of collaborators may have thrived for years without ever growing beyond Center Sandwich, but New Hampshire in the early Depression years was fortunate in having as its governor the progressive Republican John G. Winant, who was quick to recognize the economic potential of a state-wide program such as the one Mrs. Coolidge had encouraged. In 1931, he set up the Arts and Crafts Commission, and authorized it to sponsor the New Hampshire League of Arts and Crafts. With state financial assistance and a staff in Concord, the League began to coordinate the efforts of artisans and open shops throughout New Hampshire. Later renamed the League of New Hampshire Craftsmen, it continues to flourish

today. The range of goods produced and sold is far more varied and sophisticated than in the early years, and represents the efforts of craftspeople relatively new to the state as well as the "nth-generation" natives on its original roster. Still, the devotion to quality, originality, and hand workmanship remains the same.

All of the League's shops are worth browsing, but when you go to the one in Center Sandwich you are visiting some place special. Here is the birthplace of a cooperative effort, spurred by newcomers yet dependent on local human resources, that has grown beyond the lakes region to encompass the entire state.

*Above:* A quiet backwater of Lake Winnipesaukee.
CLYDE H. SMITH

*Above left:* Although more modern and less labor-intensive techniques predominate, it's possible to see haying done the traditional way in New Hampshire. Regardless of method, the job still calls for a string of clear, dry days: one makes hay while the sun shines.
CLYDE H. SMITH

*Left:* Autumn's richest New England harvest—to paraphrase Oscar Wilde, it's as useless as all great art.
CHRISTIAN HEEB

# CHAPTER SIX

# The White Mountains

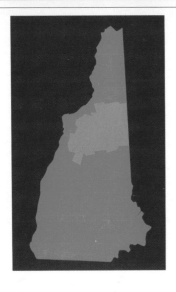

***Above:*** *The Swift River rises just north of Mt. Passaconaway in the White Mountain National Forest, and flows alongside the Kancamagus Highway to meet the Saco at Conway.*

***Facing page:*** *The summit of Mt. Chocorua, 3,475'. Here the Chief Chocorua is said to have leaped to his death, shrieking an everlasting curse at the white man.*
GEORGE WUERTHNER PHOTOS

New Hampshire draws its sense of itself from the White Mountains. Like the Indians who believed that the summit of Mt. Washington was the abode of spirits, the people of New Hampshire retain an atavistic notion that the genius of their hardiness and self-reliance is harbored in the hills beyond Winnipesaukee. They may have built ships in Portsmouth, spun cotton in Manchester, or tended cattle along the Connecticut bottom-lands, but they are proud that theirs are the fast-nesses of the Presidentials and the ring of 4,000-footers that surrounds the Pemigewasset Wilder-ness. Owning the roof of New England makes you a Yankee's Yankee.

For outsiders, the entire state of New Hampshire tends to concentrate in the White Mountains: if someone has been here once, or seen the place only in pictures, this is what he remembers. New Hampshire draws itself up to its full height north of the 44th parallel, and casts its longest shadows.

Passage between any of the other regions described in this book is more a matter of under-standing than stark geographical fact. You don't suddenly realize that you're leaving the Connecti-cut Valley and entering the watershed of the Merrimack River, or passing from the seacoast to the lakes. But when you leave Tamworth or

Center Sandwich on any of the roads headed north, it is as if you are approaching the tangible gates of a new territory. The peaks of the Sandwich Range—Sandwich Mountain, Mt. Whiteface, Mt. Passaconaway—and noble Mt. Chocorua loom ahead to isolate the easy hills of the lake country from the high places beyond.

Passaconaway and Chocorua are mountains connected to the realm of myth. The former is named for a great chief of the Penacooks. A friend to the white men, he was eventually betrayed by them and reduced to penury on his own ancestral lands. He lived to extreme old age—at his death in 1682 he was said to be 100 years old or more—and according to legend he did not die a mortal's death but was borne to the top of Mt. Washington on a sled pulled by 24 enormous wolves. At the summit, Passaconaway and his wild equipage ascended into heaven in a cloud of fire.

Chocorua (pronounced *Cho-kor-oo-way*) was a historical figure, a chief of the Pequawkets, who lived with a small remnant of his tribe near Conway about the year 1760. According to the most widely circulated version of the legend surrounding his death, he was a friend to a white man named Cornelius Campbell, who lived nearby with his family. Chocorua's son, nine or ten years old, spent much time with the Campbells. One day the little boy came home to his father sick from having eaten poisoned maple syrup put out by the Campbells for foxes, and he died. Chocorua in his grief refused to accept his son's death as an accident, and took revenge by murdering Campbell's family while the white man was away. Campbell tracked down the chief, and cornered him at the edge of the precipice on Mt. Chocorua's summit. Ordered to leap to his death or be shot, Chocorua refused to move, crying out that "the Great Spirit gave life to Chocorua and Chocorua will not throw it away at the command of the white man." Campbell shot; Chocorua fell to the ground. Raising himself on one arm, the chief spoke his dying words:

"A curse upon you, white men! May the Great Spirit curse you…Lightning blast your crops! Winds and fire destroy your dwellings! The Evil Spirit breathe death upon your cattle! Your graves

lie in the warpath of the Indian! Panthers howl and wolves fatten upon your bones! Chocorua goes to the Great Spirit—but his curse stays with the white man!"

With that, Chocorua threw himself over the edge. For many years, people in the valley west of Conway felt the curse had struck, as wolves and bears beleaguered them and their cattle died from bad water. No such evil appears to linger here

today, although the handsome, symmetrical breast of Mt. Chocorua, in sunlight or in cloud, remains a sad reminder of its legend. Myth or not, Chocorua's story stands as a metaphor for the extinction of a race.

## Into the Three Great Notches

Mt. Chocorua rises just inside the southern boundary of the White Mountain National Forest.

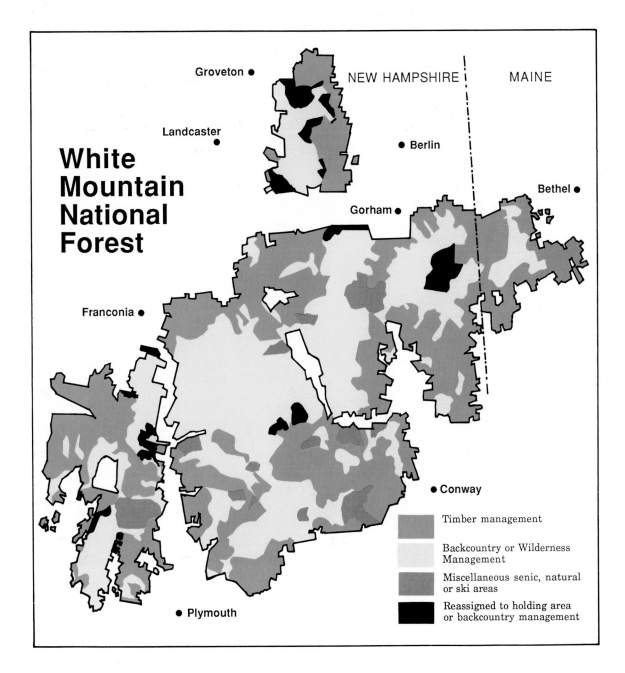

# White Mountain National Forest

Groveton ●

NEW HAMPSHIRE : MAINE

Landcaster

● Berlin

Bethel ●

Gorham ●

Franconia ●

● Conway

| | Timber management |
|---|---|
| | Backcountry or Wilderness Management |
| | Miscellaneous senic, natural or ski areas |
| | Reassigned to holding area or backcountry management |

● Plymouth

The forest was established in 1911, when the federal government appropriated funds to purchase and manage extensive tracts of New Hampshire timberland previously left to the mercy of the era's less-than-enlightened logging concerns. Today's 773,000-acre White Mountain National Forest comprises most of the north-central part of New Hampshire, and extends into western Maine as well. Logging is by no means prohibited in the forest, but is relegated to specific areas according to a U.S. Forest Service master plan. Certain other portions of the government's holdings are designated as "roadless areas," protected from timber cutting and road building. Of these, a select number of tracts, such as the Great Gulf on the eastern slopes of Mt. Washington and the vast empty quarter that surrounds the East Branch of the Pemigewasset west of Crawford Notch, are kept in a pristine state under the terms of the federal Eastern Wilderness Act. No road building, logging, permanent structure or motorized recreation is allowed in these areas, which constitute the cream of federally-protected back-country lands in the Northeast. Had today's wilderness legislation and the public pressure for its increased application existed in the 1930s, work would most likely never have begun on the Kancamagus Highway, which skirts the southern reaches of the Pemigewasset Wilderness and connects Conway with Lincoln. As it turned out, the terrain itself was stubborn in its opposition to the project and the road wasn't completed until 1959. Regardless of how you feel about whether or not it should be there, the Kancamagus makes for a beautiful drive. Just be prepared for two things. First, traffic on the Kancamagus can be horrific during peak foliage season or summer weekends. Second, its protected environs give way, at Lincoln, to a stretch of the most condo-miniumized and overdeveloped territory this side of North Conway.

The Kancamagus Highway is an anomaly in the White Mountains, in that it runs east and west. Throughout the rest of the range, the only three direct routes run north and south. Up here the passes have been called "notches" since time immemorial, and they go by the names of

Crawford, in the center; Pinkham, on the east; and Franconia, on the west.

## Crawford Notch and the Legacy of Mountain Innkeeping

Crawford Notch, which today forms the pass used by U.S. Route 302 between Bartlett and Twin Mountain, was discovered quite by accident by a moose hunter, Timothy Nash, in 1771. Nash immediately reported his find to Governor John Wentworth, who was interested in developing roads into the New Hampshire interior. The governor was skeptical, but agreed to give Nash a tract of land at the northern end of the notch if the backwoodsman could bring a horse south to Portsmouth along the route he had described. In what must have been one of the most comical and exhausting treks in White Mountain history, Nash and a friend named Benjamin Sawyer rode, pushed and cajoled a farm horse through Crawford Notch, sometimes using a rope sling to lower the animal over ledges and down steep banks. Nash and Sawyer got their land grant, and New Hampshire had a wilderness pass to develop through the White Mountains to the upper Connecticut Valley. In 1803, the route through Crawford Notch became part of the state's Tenth Turnpike.

Crawford Notch got its name from the family of Abel and Hannah Crawford, who settled on the notch road in 1792 and raised nine children in the wilderness. Crawford must have felt that his home still needed a few more people in it, since he soon opened it to travelers as the Mount Crawford House. This was the first hostelry in the notch, and in its day one of the most famous in New England. The Mount Crawford House was where you stayed if you were heading through the center of the White Mountains, and if you had come to visit the mountains themselves Abel Crawford and his strapping son Ethan Allen Crawford would leave their tavern hearth and hire on as your guides. In 1819, father and son built the Crawford Trail east from their inn to the summit of Mount Washington; two years later, Ethan Allen Crawford blazed a more direct trail to the top over the route followed decades later by the Cog Railway. By

1823, the "Giant of the Hills," as the younger Crawford was called, had built a cluster of huts on the barren and windy Mt. Washington summit. Anyone he guided to the top was doubtless treated to the story of how he and his comrades had stood there and named the Presidentials, and just as surely the rum came out for a reprise of the christening. Those were the days before guide-

**Top:** *The automobiles suggest that this is the 1930s; the place is the majestic Crawford House. Built in 1859 on the site of a smaller hotel, it lasted until 1977 before succumbing—like its predecessor—to fire.* COURTESY NEW HAMPSHIRE HISTORICAL SOCIETY **Left:** *A road crew works late to keep Franconia accessible to the outside world.* CLYDE H. SMITH **Right:** *A saw-whet owl, photographed at Hancock.* TED LEVIN

books lectured hikers about alcohol dilating the blood vessels.

The time of Abel and Ethan Allen Crawford and their succession of inns in Crawford Notch was the pioneer era of White Mountain trailblazing and hotelkeeping, described in fascinating detail in the *History of the White Mountains* published in 1846, the year of the younger man's death, by his wife Lucy Crawford. (Abel Crawford died at 85 in 1850, having served in the state legislature during his last years.) Before long the notch would become as much a destination as a means of passage, and in so doing it made the White

Mountains the first mountains to be "discovered" by the American people and adopted as a realm of aesthetic uplift rather than disparaged as an inconvenience to settlement. Our appreciation of mountains began not with the Rockies or Tetons or even the Adirondacks, but with the hills of New Hampshire. Their only possible rival in this regard are the Catskills of New York.

Stagecoaches brought guests to the original Mount Crawford House, open until 1876; to the Mount Washington House (expanded from an inn built by Ethan Allen Crawford in 1825); and to its successor, the capacious Fabyan House, built in

1873 and destroyed by fire in 1951. The Crawford House, begun by Abel Crawford's son Tom and finished by new owners in 1852, burned in 1859 but was immediately rebuilt to survive for more than 120 years. This last Crawford House was a great E-shaped building that could house up to 400 guests. It stood at an elevation of 2,000' on a height of land dividing the Saco and Ammonoosuc watersheds, and its broad verandah commanded one of the notch's finest views. It burned to the ground in 1977 leaving only the nearby railroad station on Route 302. The station, once used almost exclusively in season by Crawford House guests, today serves as a bookstore and information center operated by the Appalachian Mountain Club.

That little Victorian depot may seem lost without its grand hotel, but it is in itself a monument to one of the White Mountains' boldest human achievements. It was the railroad, the impossible railroad through Crawford Notch, that ushered in the golden age of mountain resort hotels.

The laying of track between North Conway and Fabyan, at the northern entrance to Crawford Notch, has been cited as the most difficult railroad construction job in New Hampshire. It was undertaken in the late 1880s by two brothers, Samuel and John Anderson, and their Portland and Ogdensburg Railroad Company. John Anderson was chief engineer of the firm, responsible for the bold 500′ trestle across Frankenstein Gulf and the bridge spanning 100′-deep Willey Brook Ravine. Between North Conway and Fabyan, a distance of 30 miles, the railroad climbed 1,369′; over the nine miles leading north to the Crawford House, the tracks ascended 116′ to the mile. The trip from North Conway to the Crawford House took an hour and a half when the road was opened. That's 27 miles at 18 mph, not bad for terrain that had required lowering a horse on ropes just a century before. And no passenger ever complained about the view.

The Portland and Ogdensburg went into receivership in 1887, after which it was picked up by the Maine Central and operated as a passenger line well into this century. Finally, bus and automobile travel on improved roads made passenger rail service in the mountains outmoded—with one notable exception, as we'll see later.

Among the great, rambling hotels of the White Mountains, perhaps the most famous of all is the largest still in operation: the Mount Washington Hotel in Bretton Woods. The snow-white, red-roofed Mount Washington nestles majestically against the western slopes of its namesake peak, looking as if it were about to welcome its traditional complement of summer-long guests with servants and steamer trunks, some arriving in their private railroad cars. Today's clientele arrives with

far less fanfare, but they still enjoy the privilege of having idle daytrippers excluded from their midst. If you want to go to the Mount Washington Hotel just to look around, you'll have to pay a small fee at the gate.

This last of the mountains' *grandes dames* was built in 1902, and dedicated with a ball to which Ethan Allen Crawford III was invited. The big, Y-shaped hotel (it currently offers 207 rooms and suites) was designed to be the centerpiece of a fully-equipped playland, and so it remains— there are tennis courts, a golf course, bridle trails, two heated pools, and sumptuous restaurants. Lodgings at the Mount Washington, available between May and October, even come with a bit

*Above:* The Mount Washington Hotel, at Bretton Woods, is the grand survivor of the glory days of White Mountains innkeeping. CHRISTIAN HEEB

*Facing page, left:* Beginning in 1887 and lasting into the 1930s, the White Mountains hotels kept up the tradition of "Gala Day Coaching Parade" each August 22. Competition among hostelries was keen, with a coveted prize awarded to the most grandly-decorated coach.
*Right:* Named not for its fright value but for an Ohio artist who summered in the mountains, the Frankenstein Trestle still is one of the more hair-raising sections of the Mt. Washington Cog Railway.
IMAGES COURTESY OF NEW HAMPSHIRE HISTORICAL SOCIETY

of world history. In 1944, this was the site of the 44-nation Bretton Woods Conference that based the international monetary structure on the U.S. dollar. Two hundred of your own dollars should do very nicely for a double, per night.

## Pinkham Notch

Pinkham Notch, named for Joseph Pinkham who settled here in 1790, constitutes the eastern pass around the massif of the Presidential Range. Route 16 strikes for the notch as it proceeds north out of North Conway, up through Glen and Jackson. You'll have to turn left at the covered bridge to see Jackson village, a tidy little settlement with comfortable inns, built around a green at the foot of the Wildcat Brook rapids.

Past Jackson the notch proper begins, walled in on the west by the slopes of Mt. Eisenhower, Mt. Franklin and Mt. Washington itself; and on the east by the curving phalanx of North, South and Middle Carter Mountains and Carter Dome, all rising above 4,000′. The eastern slope of Mt. Washington is the side tackled by the famous Auto Road, of which more later. It is also the side tackled by the nerviest skiers in the East (should we say the world?), who come here to accept the challenge of Tuckerman Ravine. Named for the 19th-century botanist Dr. Edward Tuckerman, the ravine is technically a cirque, a glacially-scooped basin indented like a natural amphitheater in the flank of Mt. Washington. Ever since the early days of skiing in New Hampshire in the 1930s, the true

**Above, left:** *Red spruce at timberline: Mt. Kearsarge.* GEORGE WUERTHNER
**Right:** *Feathery rime ice covers the rocky summit of Mount Washington, at 6,288′ the highest point in the northeastern United States.* TOM TILL

**Facing page, top:** *A contrast in techniques: at right, the great Austrian instructor Hannes Schneider executes a flashy turn in the days of wooden skis and leather boots.* COURTESY NEW HAMPSHIRE HISTORICAL SOCIETY *At left, a modern skier kicks up his heels at Wildcat Mountain.* CLYDE H. SMITH
**Bottom:** *Morning mist rises on the Ammonoosuc River near Swiftwater, on the western fringes of the White Mountain National Forest.* JEFF GNASS

diehards have ventured on foot from the Appalachian Mountain Club camp on the notch floor to ascend the steep upper rim of the basin—the headwall at Tuckerman, as it is reverentially known—and ski down. The sport doesn't begin here until after avalanche season, usually mid- or late April, and it can last into July. The drop is roughly 1,000′, growing ever steeper near the top, and there never has been a lift or tow. In 1987, the Mt. Washington Cog Railway announced plans to begin winter service to the top of the headwall. There were howls from traditionalists, and a flat denial of a guide permit from the U.S. Forest Service, which maintained that easy access would invite too many skiers short on the necessary respect for Tuckerman. If you couldn't see what it was like as you were walking up, the reasoning went, you wouldn't know what you were in for on the way down. When last heard from, the railway people were talking about simply running the winter trains as a transportation service, without pretense of guiding skiers. Passengers, of course, would be allowed to bring skis.

Only a tiny fraction of the people who come to New Hampshire to ski ever attempt Tuckerman Ravine. For the majority, a tremendous infrastructure of ski areas and service businesses has sprung up since the days when Carroll Reed set up America's first open-enrollment ski school at the Eastern Slope Inn in North Conway in 1936. Reed, founder of the skiwear and sports clothes business that still thrives in North Conway, hired former Austrian Army ski instructor Hannes Schneider to run his school, and Schneider trained a generation of American recreational skiers. The B&M Railroad did its part by running its famous "snow trains" from Boston to North Conway, beginning in 1931. Departing the city before dawn, the trains would be met by the sleighs, buses and station wagons of the inns and early ski resorts.

The snow trains have been gone now for more than 30 years. Today's skiers travel by car up Route 16 and Interstate 93, and ascend the slopes not by rope tow but by the chairlifts, tramways and gondolas of sprawling areas such as Mount Cranmore and Wildcat, in the North Conway-Jackson area; Cannon Mountain in Franconia

*Above: The old depot at North Conway, a perfect Victorian confection. No longer a main-line stop, the station still is served by excursion trains in the summer and fall.* CHRISTIAN HEEB

*Facing page, top: No Velcro here: this hardy group is taking its midday rest at the Appalachian Mountain Club's Madison Springs hut, circa 1900. Built in 1888 at a cost of about $770, the hut was destroyed by fire in 1940. It since has been replaced by a larger facility.*
COURTESY APPALACHIAN MOUNTAIN CLUB

*Left: A winter camp above Tuckerman Ravine on Mount Washington. At least these climbers expected winter—the mountain's reputation for danger arises from its capricious weather in other seasons.*
CLYDE H. SMITH

*Right: Lake of the Clouds, above treeline on Mount Washington. This is the site of Appalachian Mountain Club's most popular mountain hut.* IAN J. ADAMS

Notch; Attitash, west of North Conway; and the big Waterville Valley and Loon Mountain complexes east and south of Lincoln. The impact of these enormous enterprises on the local economy has been impressive, but no less significant is their power to alter the physical appearance of the mountain towns. Skiers have to be fed, clothed, housed and entertained, and the profusion of establishments doing the job has brought the phenomenon of strip development to communities that were neat, self-contained villages just a few decades ago. North Conway is the most striking example: as late as the mid-1960s, a visitor passed little more than a couple of gas stations and a handful of restaurants on the way into town from the south, and saw even less on the northern, Pinkham Notch, side of the village. Today, the

southern approaches to North Conway begin at Conway, and are lined with designer clothes outlets and fast-food joints. The town itself is a relief, the calm eye of the storm, where the colonnaded Eastern Slope Inn and the delightful, triple-towered Victorian train station still dominate.

Past Jackson, where the woods take over, the development strictures of the White Mountain National Forest take over as well. Along with the national forest and its Forest Service managers, the most important fact of life in this territory is the Appalachian Mountain Club (AMC). Fact of life? By now it's a force of nature, having predated the National Forest by more than 30 years. The AMC was founded in 1876 by a group of Bostonians interested in hiking, climbing and the natural history of the mountains at their northern doorstep. (Despite the organization's name, its prime focus always has been the White Mountains.) In 1888, the Club built the first of its huts at Madison Springs, in a col, or saddle, above the walls of Madison Gulf between Mt. Madison and Mt. Adams. Madison Springs, replaced after a fire in 1941, remains the northernmost in what became a string of eight AMC huts, not counting the base camp and North Country headquarters of the Club at Pinkham Notch. The others, completed between 1904 and 1965, are Carter Notch, east of Pinkham between Wildcat Mountain and Carter Dome; Lakes of the Clouds, above treeline at the 5,000' level on Mt. Washington; Mizpah Spring, on Mt. Clinton; Zealand Falls and Galehead, on the northern fringes of the Pemigewasset Wilderness; and Lonesome Lake, in Franconia Notch below the Old Man of the Mountains. The huts are between three and six miles apart—approximately one day's mountain hiking—and all offer meals and bunk space.

Having gotten into the room-and-board business by establishing this European-style chain of hikers' accommodations in the White Mountains, the AMC quite naturally found itself involved in maintaining the network of trails that links the huts with each other and with the base of operations at Pinkham. The trails are an important aspect of back-country management; their good condition and sustained use, in combination with the provision of permanent facilities at the huts, enables large numbers of hikers to traverse the mountains without causing cumulative ecological damage. If all the people seeking to enjoy the alpine meadows at Lakes of the Clouds or the solemn views of the Pemigewasset Wilderness at Galehead were forced to rely on random campsites and a haphazard system of trails, the terrain would be trampled flat and the forest would be picked as clean of firewood as the delta of the Ganges.

As an outgrowth of its long involvement with the trails and its experience with the management of back-country recreation, the Appalachian Mountain Club has evolved an informal yet deeply rooted position of co-stewardship with the Forest Service in the White Mountains. The AMC is involved in environmental research and occasional lobbying, in the training of volunteers, and in instructional programs ranging from rock climbing to telemark skiing to whitewater canoeing. Its publishing arm produces the most detailed guidebooks to the region, including the oft-revised *White Mountain Guide*. Along with simply being there and running the huts, though, the most important aspect of the AMC's role in the White Mountains is the one people would hope never to need: wilderness search and rescue (SAR). The White Mountains are not terribly high, as the world's mountains go, but they are extremely rugged and subject to horrific reverses in weather, even in summer. Not everyone comes properly prepared in experience and equipment, and even those who do can run afoul of climate and terrain.

The AMC maintains a search-and-rescue staff of roughly 30 to 40 trained volunteers in winter, and 100 in summer. The core of this group is the "notchwatchers," on 24-hour duty at Pinkham. They may receive reports of back-country situations requiring emergency attention from individuals, or through the New Hampshire Fish and Game Department or the U.S. Forest Service; both government organizations rely upon AMC Search and Rescue to supplement their own efforts. Once having checked in with the authorities, the Pinkham-based teams swing into action.

On a busy Saturday afternoon during the AMC's fall "Town Meeting" at Pinkham, I tracked

**Above:** *A horse-drawn hay wagon pauses on a valley road in the White Mountains.*
**Right:** *Autumn in the valley, winter above: Mount Washington framed by birches.* GERARD LEMMO PHOTOS

**Facing page:** *Hoarfrost in June on the summit of Mount Washington.* NONA BAUER

down Peter Crane, assistant manager of the camp. Crane spent two and a half years as a "notch-watcher," and before that worked in search-and-rescue field operations; today, he is responsible for coordinating the Club's role in all SAR work. "Things have been quiet," Crane remarked. "In 1987, through late October, we had about 25 missions of varying complexity, including an ice-climbing accident in Huntington Ravine that required a multiple evacuation. In the summer, most of our litter carries are fairly straightfor-ward—broken legs, ankle injuries—but things get a little more complicated in winter, with the occasional ice climbing trauma and Tuckerman ski accidents."

Crane, a pleasant-spoken man with that Ivy-League appearance that seems to survive in AMC

circles, has been at this business a long time. I asked him about the most trying situation he had been involved in. He leaned over his big desk on the mezzanine above the Pinkham hubbub, thought for a moment, and told me about the death of MacDonald Barr, from hypothermia, on Mt. Madison in late August 1986.

"I was manning the radio at Pinkham when the call came in from Madison Springs. Three people—a sixty-year-old man, his thirteen-year-old son and another teenage boy—had been hiking near the summit of Mt. Madison. The weather was cold and blustery, with temperatures in the thirties and strong gusts driving the rain sideways. At about six in the evening the older boy had come stumbling into the hut, saying the father and son both needed help.

"The full seriousness of the matter was not clear from the boy's report. One hut crew member went out, with blankets, hats and jackets and hot cocoa. He got to the son, Travis Barr, who told him that his father, up near the summit, needed help more than he did. So the hutman made sure the boy was warm and comfortable, and went on towards the summit. Now the rain was turning to sleet, and the winds were over seventy miles an hour.

"The hutman found MacDonald Barr in an irrational and combative stage of hypothermia. He fought off all attempts to assist him; he wouldn't take a jacket or cocoa." (Barr had been wearing a sweater and light windbreaker; he had no hat or gloves.) "The hutman called Pinkham on his mobile radio, and we got a team under way to Madison Springs at eight o'clock. Barr was too much for one man to handle, so the hutman went down to Travis, who was only a fifth of a mile from the hut, got help, and brought the boy in.

"By now it was almost nine o'clock, and it was dark. There were ice pellets, rain, and fog, and the winds on Mt. Washington were averaging almost eighty miles an hour. There was no hope, under those conditions, of reaching MacDonald Barr on the summit of Madison. A team left Madison Springs at seven the next morning, and found him half an hour later. They pronounced him dead at Androscoggin Valley Hospital.

"This is the most frustrating thing someone in this place can get involved in. As much as we want to help people, there are times when weather, terrain and darkness defeat our intentions."

## Up on Mt. Washington

The weather conditions that combined to kill MacDonald Barr occurred in August, in a place on the same latitude as Minneapolis and with an altitude scarcely higher than the streets of Denver. But these comparisons mean nothing in the Presidential Range, where the climate is as fierce and capricious as anywhere in the United States. The oft-repeated cliche is that Mt. Washington has "the worst weather in the world," and in terms of sheer dramatic changeability this probably is true. The South Pole just stays consistently miserable;

nobody freezes there because they dressed for a lark in 70° weather and got caught in an ice storm.

If there is a single instance that has contributed more than any other to Mt. Washington's reputation for climatic extremes, it is the one that occurred on Thursday, April 12, 1934. On that day the instruments at the summit's Mount Washington Observatory recorded a wind speed of 231 mph, the greatest ever documented on the planet.

"There was a tremendous pressure differential that day," explains Guy Gosselin, who serves today as director of the Observatory. "There was a deep low to the southeast, and a high-pressure region to the northwest. The conditions have never been exactly duplicated. We've never had a wind speed higher than 200 mph since then,

although it's been recorded at 196. I would expect it may approach the record again someday."

I had hoped to meet Gosselin on the summit, at the fine new concrete Sherman Adams Building erected in 1980 to replace the Observatory's old headquarters, the "strongest wooden building in the world." But there were 8″ of snow on the summit that October day, and the Auto Road was closed. Not that the director himself wouldn't be headed up soon; he had a four-wheel-drive pickup with tire chains, and if worse came to worst there was always the tracked LMC Sprite that makes the run for crew changes each Wednesday. But we talked in the big kitchen of Gosselin's house in Gorham, just 10 miles from the summit, where there was still a leaf or two on the

**Above:** *Traction gears firmly enmeshed in a rack between the rails, doughty locomotives of the Mt. Washington Cog Railway work their way to the summit.* CLYDE H. SMITH

**Facing page:** *Dating back to stagecoach days, the Mt. Washington Auto Road long has been open to private vehicles.* GERARD LEMMO

kind of wind; you just have to crawl on the ground. You could stand up and lean into a high wind if it were steady, but it keeps changing and you'd always be falling down. We have a 'Century Club' among our staff. It includes anyone who has gone out to get the precipitation can in winds over 100 mph."

There is a lot more to the Mount Washington Observatory's mission than recording superlative wind speeds. The private-sector institution, founded in 1932 after years of sporadic weather research on the mountain, sells its services to the U.S. Weather Service, the Army Corps of Engineers' Cold Regions Research and Engineering Laboratories in Hanover, and a variety of corporate and government clients interested in weather patterns and exposure tests of materials. There's also a long-standing relationship with the University of New Hampshire, with current efforts focused on documenting bombardment of the summit with low-energy neutrons, a by-product of cosmic rays in the upper atmosphere.

Instruments at the summit record precipitation, barometric pressure, temperature, dewpoint, relative humidity and, of course, wind speed and direction. Observers also make analyses of clouds, determining such factors as water content and median droplet diameter—all easy to do when the cloud is what you walk into when you open the observatory door. "Having a permanent station above 6,000' means getting a picture of the weather there on a constant basis," Gosselin points out. "The instruments are going all the time. It's not like a balloon."

Also unlike a balloon, the Mount Washington Observatory is staffed by human beings. In the winter when no one else comes to the summit, they are psychological kinsmen, in many ways, of lighthouse keepers and astronauts. "There's no question but that the mountain works on people in certain ways," Gosselin admits, "but most of the people we hire come with a natural propensity for working in an isolated area. They have to be mature, and they have to have a sense of humor. We can choose the sort of person that will work well, since we always have more applicants than we have openings."

trees and the only concession to weather was another log on the fire.

"The strongest wind I've ever seen on the summit was 184 mph," recalled Gosselin, who came to the Observatory in 1961 and learned meteorology on the job. He is a bearded man in a wool shirt, and he speaks in the moderate tones of a data-collector. "When they were working on the new building, we had gusts over 180. One blew over a semitrailer that had been detached from its cab and used for storage. Then the eye of the storm passed. The wind reversed and picked the trailer right back up. It's possible to go out in that

Perhaps that's because word gets around that there's more to life at the top of New England than just recording professional observations. Mt. Washington isn't all whiteouts and fog and howling winds. There are pellucid mornings when you can see Portland Harbor, 75 miles away, and watch the ships with your binoculars. Under the best circumstances you can see Mt. Mansfield in Vermont, Whiteface and Mt. Marcy in the Adirondacks (Marcy is 139 miles away), and even far distant peaks that "loom" disembodied above the horizon when the atmosphere acts as a lens. One observer kept a record of how many lighthouses he could see at night. There are also visual phenomena such as the Brocken Specter, in which fog and a setting sun conspire to project your own ghostly figure on a point hundreds of feet away, allowing you to wave at yourself and receive a wave in return. At times the green flash will come at sunset. And if you are very lucky—it happens maybe eight or 10 times a year, Gosselin figures—dawn will reveal a piercingly bright ribbon of silver, as the sun glances for an instant off the distant Atlantic Ocean.

## Wheels to the Top

Especially in Appalachian Mountain Club circles, the honorable way to get to the top of Mt. Washington is on foot. But there are two other time-honored means of reaching the summit, the Auto Road and the Mt. Washington Cog Railway.

The Auto Road, originally the "Carriage Road," was completed in 1861 after seven years of off-and-on labor involving horses, oxen and human muscle. The eight-mile route to the top was originally traversed by stout Concord coaches, pulled by eight horses each, which left from the old Glen House in Pinkham Notch. Private auto travel began in 1908, and in 1912 the company operating the road began using gasoline-powered coaches to carry passengers disinclined to trust their own driving skills and hotel guests who had left their Pierce-Arrows at home.

Today the Auto Road is safe and smoothly graded, and open between May and October for travel via motor coach or private car. While nosing heavenward at your stately, careful pace, think

about Bill Rutan. He set the speed record the last time a race to the top was held, in 1961. Driving a homemade cross between a Volkswagen and a Porsche, Rutan made the eight-mile trip in nine minutes and 13 seconds.

The Cog Railway ascends from Crawford Notch, on the other side of Mt. Washington. A marvelous piece of 19th-century technology, the railway was conceived in 1852 by Sylvester Marsh, a Littleton native who had made his money in meat packing. Although Marsh's receipt of an 1858 state charter to build his railroad to the summit prompted one legislator to comment that he should also be permitted to lay tracks to the moon, the sharply-graded (as steep as 37.4 percent) line was completed by 1869. No less impressive than the engineering of the road—most of which is carried on trestles—is the design of the

little steam engines that chuff heroically to the top. The basic design was the work of Walter Aiken of Franklin, New Hampshire. It involves a notched rack laid centrally between the two rails, and a corresponding "cog," or toothed gear, driven by the engine and fitting into the rack. The simple adhesion that allows trains to move forward on level track would never have worked with these grades. All of the locomotives that succeeded the original, "Old Peppersass" (still on display at the base station), follow the same principle. The engines in use today still are steam-powered, and are fitted with inclined boilers that compensate for the angle of the grades—hence their weary, "buckled" look when they are on level ground. The three-mile trip up the mountain on this oldest of the world's cog railways takes about an hour and 15 minutes, with passengers riding ahead of

the locomotive (behind on the way down) in open or closed coaches.

## The Natural Wonders of Franconia Notch

Franconia, the westernmost of the White Mountain notches, is the home of New Hampshire's craggy-browed symbol, the naturally-formed stone face known as the Old Man of the Mountains. Although white men knew about the pass between present-day Lincoln and Franconia in the late 18th century, its first popular recognition usually is associated with the 1805 discovery of the Old Man himself. According to the most widely-accepted account, this came about when Francis Whitcomb and Luke Brooks, surveyors working on the first road through the notch, glanced up at Cannon Mountain and beheld the stone visage while washing their hands in what has since been named Profile Lake. It isn't hard to understand how the 48' face could have gone undiscovered by previous visitors to the notch; it juts from a point high on the mountain, and a clear view of it requires a vantage point at just the right place below. Nowadays this isn't very difficult, as signs indicating a turnoff on Interstate 93 say "Old Man Viewing" and point straight to a parking lot complete with rest rooms. (What do people who have never heard of the face think when they see that sign?) This stretch of interstate, incidentally, represents a compromise to a fierce and complicated debate waged from the late 1960s into the early 1980s over how to connect the loose ends of I-93 at either end of Franconia Notch. Environmentalists wanted a two-lane highway; the government wanted to finish the four-lane interstate. The road you drive today is a hybrid, a mini-interstate accepted as a compromise.

One of the concerns voiced during the dispute over highway construction was that the vibrations of high-speed traffic might eventually shake loose the granite slabs that make up the stone face. While this theory never was given much credence, the Old Man's friends have been worried enough about frost damage to brace the three ledges that form the forehead, nose, and chin of the profile with anchor irons and cables. The earliest work of this kind was done in 1916,

and since has been reinforced. Losing the Old Man of the Mountains would be unthinkable. More than just a state icon, it was the inspiration for the famous remark about God advertising the making of men in New Hampshire, and of Hawthorne's tale "The Great Stone Face." In the story, a boy named Ernest grows to manhood in the shadow of the profile, always looking for a man with the same noble features. At tale's end, it is Ernest himself whose kindliness and wisdom lead him, as an old man, to resemble the Great Stone Face.

Scarcely five miles south of the Old Man, on the eastern side of the road, is the second great natural formation of Franconia Notch. This is the Flume, formed by Flume Brook over the course of countless millenia. The rock here is granite, riven by intrusions of molten lava hardened into basalt dikes. By constantly wearing away at the dike over which it flowed on its way to the Pemigewasset, Flume Brook carved this deep chasm between 70′ granite walls. There is a walkway beside the stream, within the walls of the Flume. Lucy Crawford's description still rings true as you make your way along the path: "At all times there is quite a dampness as you pass through this fissure almost causing a chilly sensation to creep over the whole system; most of the ledge upon both sides is covered with moss and presents a cold dreary appearance even at noonday in summer."

On the other hand, Aunt Jess Guernsey thought it was rather pretty. She was the 93-year-old woman who discovered the Flume one day in 1803, when she was out fishing.

*Above:* The Old Man of the Mountains. CHRISTIAN HEEB
*Left:* Robert Frost, before he became a white-haired eminence. The poet lived for five years on a farm in Franconia; his property is open to the public in summer, and is the site of an artist-in-residence program each year. COURTESY NEW HAMPSHIRE HISTORICAL SOCIETY

*Facing page:* Walking along the Flume, Franconia Notch. Flume Brook found the softer rock in this formation, and worked its way deeper over the millena. JOHN J. SMITH

# CHAPTER SEVEN

# The North Country

**Right:** *The sun breaks through haze over the Connecticut Lakes. From here, New England's longest river begins its run to Long Island Sound.* CLYDE H. SMITH

**Facing page, top:** *The towering stacks of the James River Corp. dominate the horizon as well as the economy of Berlin. Pulpwood and paper have been mainstays of this North Country outpost.* CHRISTIAN HEEB

**Bottom:** *Lily pads on Lake Umbagog, source of the Androscoggin River.* TED LEVIN

The road from Pinkham Notch descends quickly to the valley of the wild Androscoggin, leaving the White Mountain National Forest at Gorham. The approach from here to Berlin (accent on the first syllable) is nothing like the approach to North Conway, on the other side of the mountains. Here, at the threshhold of the North Country, the taut illusion of gentrification snaps, and you are back in real life. North Conway sells designer ski pants. Berlin sells hunting pants.

Berlin also makes paper, miles of it, as you will immediately realize if you are downwind of the mills. This is the North Country headquarters of the James River Corporation, largest purchaser of pulp and largest independent manufacturer of specialty papers in the United States. James River is a big name in Berlin, though not an old one. The company bought the Brown Company (originally the Berlin Company), Berlin's mainstay for over a century, in 1980. But the business is the same: out of the North Country's sea of conifers comes the raw material, and out of Berlin comes paper. Newsprint is a major item; another is paper toweling. Anyone who has ever been in a public washroom is probably familiar with the name "Nibroc." The name is a reversal of the spelling of Corbin, the Brown Company man who invented it.

Berlin, seat of Coös County, is a company town with the company on one side of the Androscoggin and the town on the other. From just about anywhere on Main Street, which parallels the swift, rocky river, you can look across at the Titan stacks of James River; at one point, they stand opposite the spire of the Roman Catholic church on its side of the rapids, and you think about how many of the valley's lives have been defined along this axis. In large part they have been French lives, as a reading of the names on Main Street's signs will tell. There are other reminders of Canada as well: every Saturday at Melissa's Country Kitchen, the specialty is home-baked beans. You know you have passed beyond the land of downcountry Yankees into French-Canadian country when you see people eating beans at breakfast, and not just for supper. Like the big, hot loaves of white bread cooling at the back of Melissa's restaurant, baked beans are a

*Above:* Main Street, Lancaster. Remove the automobiles, and the year might be 1910. GEORGE WUERTHNER

*Right:* A skidder operator takes hold of a clutch of white pine logs. Mechanization in the form of skidders, trucks and chainsaws long since ended the logging era of axes, two-man saws and the great river drives. TED LEVIN

*Facing page, left:* Sunset on the Androscoggin at Shelburne, near the Maine border. JOHN J. SMITH

*Right:* A hiker looks down into Dixville Notch, where the magnificent Balsams resort stands alongside Lake Gloriette. CLYDE H. SMITH

throwback to the cuisine of the Québecois *habitants* on the farms and in the logging camps.

Logging camp—the words conjure a world of strong men and damp steaming wool, ringing axes, potbellied stoves and daily mountains of carbohydrates for calories to bring the timber down. The old-style camps—at one time there were more than 40 spread across the Brown Company's holdings—are all but gone now; many more loggers live at home. Gone too are the great river drives. Back in the early part of this century, timber companies bought land partly with an eye toward the trees it contained, and partly because of its waterways and where they led. Brown, for instance, had to get its logs into the tributaries of the Androscoggin, so the drive could end at the

mills of Berlin. As pulpwood became the mainstay of the industry, logs could be cut to shorter lengths, and floated down smaller streams. Lake Umbagog, at the head of the Androscoggin, was the great collecting point. Each spring, when melting snows raised the water levels, the timber gathered at Umbagog would be herded down the Androscoggin by men with caulked boots and the long, jam-breaking peaveys or "cant dogs." At the finish of a drive and the winter in the woods that preceded it, a town like Berlin played host to an enthusiastic group of pent-up revelers, much the way Dodge City did at the end of a cattle drive. You'd never know it to look at the place today, but it once had a reputation as something of a fleshpot.

## Northernmost of the Great Resorts

Life in the forested arm of New Hampshire that reaches north of the White Mountains hasn't always been a matter of hard work in the woods and a quick spree in Berlin. In 1873, just around the time the mills in Berlin were beginning to run strong, the Parsons family in far-northern Dixville Notch opened a 50-guest summer hotel named The Balsams. By 1917, The Balsams was a palatial 400-guest establishment to rival any of the resorts in the White Mountains proper. Land acquisitions, largely made by purchase from the Brown Paper Company, increased the size of The Balsams' domain to 15,000 acres.

Like its only large remaining competitor, the Mount Washington Hotel, The Balsams fell on

hard times toward mid-century only to be revived by a fresh infusion of capital in the postwar years. What most Balsams guests don't know is that the owner's fortune derives from a rubber-products company that he has unobtrusively moved to a cluster of buildings behind the hotel. The important thing is that he has kept intact that 15,000-acre fiefdom, which makes a perfect setting for the hotel, its ski area and its two golf courses. (The 18-hole golf course, on a plateau above the hotel and Lake Gloriette, has what must be the best views from any links in the land.) All in all, the effect is of a grand hotel in the midst of its private wilderness area.

I remember the first time I saw The Balsams, back when all I knew about Dixville Notch was that it's where New Hampshire's earliest voters cast their ballots every four years on primary and election nights. I was driving on Route 26, which crosses the northern tip of New Hampshire from Colebrook to Lake Umbagog without having much to do with civilization. If you round a bend and come upon a farmhouse, you take notice. At Dixville Notch the two-lane blacktop makes a pronounced dip and turn, and slabs along the steep side of a narrow valley. It was right at this point that the lake caught my eye, off to the left—and alongside it, an immense stucco building with a red tile roof and white wooden wings. I had no idea that the place existed, or that there was anything larger than a two-bay gas station between Colebrook and the Maine border. I looked back at the road, and half expected the red roofs and swimming pool to be gone when I looked back. It didn't just seem out of place, but out of time.

## The Indian Stream Republic

If it seems strange that the North Country of New Hampshire harbors a 15,000-acre tract that constitutes a virtual realm unto itself, consider the fact that these quiet forests once sheltered an actual independent republic—at least, one that was independent in its own eyes.

Pittsburg, the northernmost (and in *area* the largest) town in New Hampshire, was once the location of this smallest of republics. Its separation from neighboring authorities came about because of difficulties in agreeing upon a boundary between the United States and Canada in the years after the Revolution. In keeping with the terms of the Treaty of Paris, both sides understood that the border was to be the most northwestern of the sources of the Connecticut River. But the Canadians recognized the source as being the river that links the chain of Connecticut Lakes, while the United States looked to Indian Stream, farther west, as the river's true source.

In 1831, there were 360 settlers living in the disputed territory. Things came to a head that year when the local Canadian authorities tried to press Indian Stream men into the army, while New Hampshire levied an import duty on any of their produce shipped into Coös County proper. A plague on both your houses, the backwoodsmen declared, and in the summer of 1832 they met at their schoolhouse to establish the Republic of Indian Stream. The constitution was a masterpiece of democratic simplicity. Every voter was a member of the legislature, and there was a five-man executive council whose chairman was the president of Indian Stream. There were courts, a provision for constitutional amendment by a two-thirds vote of the legislature, and a 40-man militia.

Trouble came to the Indian Stream Republic from within and without. Both the U.S. and Canada continued to assert their sovereignty over the tiny domain, and to make matters worse there were factions within Indian Stream that leaned in each direction. At the middle were some brave, Athenian-spirited individuals who still wanted to go it alone. Matters deteriorated to the point of violence, at which point the New Hampshire militia stepped in to strongly suggest union with the Granite State. This was in 1835. Five years later, with most of the Canadian sympathizers having moved across the border, the Indian Stream territory formally became the town of Pittsburg. In 1842, U.S. Secretary of State Daniel Webster and Britain's Lord Ashburton settled the international boundary at Hall's Stream—slightly west of Indian Stream—which is more or less where it stands today.

## End of the Line

Pittsburg is where New Hampshire ends. The state comes to a point and disappears from the map, not in a flourish of cities and rich farms but in a whisper of pines. The town is a vast, silent forest. There can't be many more people in the tiny village than there were in the days of Indian Stream, except in summer when the fishermen come. There are no Balsams or Mount Washington hotels here, only the cabins that the fishermen rent. They fit the place well, even the plainest of them with their weary refrigerators and screen doors that let the midgies in. One of my best New Hampshire nights was spent in such a cabin on Back Lake, where a candlelight reading of Robert Frost's "The Witch of Coös" was serendipitously prefaced by the ghostly ululations of the loons.

I hired a guide the next morning and went fishing. We were out on his boat on the First Connecticut Lake, and he was showing me how to troll for lake trout with a fly rod. It's an odd

*Above:* Autumn foliage on a back road near Dixville Notch. The quality of each fall's display depends on a number of factors, not the least of which is the preceding season's rainfall pattern. JEFF GNASS

*Facing page:* Beaver Brook Falls spills down a mountain ledge near Colebrook. GEORGE WUERTHNER

*Above:* The bandstand on the town common at Whitefield, done up for the holidays. CLYDE H. SMITH
*Right:* Not all maple syrup comes from Vermont. BRUCE BERG

*Facing page:* A fish rises on the Third Connecticut Lake. It may be an American or a Canadian fish; the border bisects this northernmost lake in the chain. CLYDE H. SMITH

business, in which you put a streamer on your leader and let out a great deal of line. I had never heard of it before. The guide was an immensely fat man of about 35, who earns his living in winter by tying flies and in summer by taking flatlanders out to fish with them. He talked about living in Pittsburg with the zeal of a man who had escaped to this place.

"Where are you from?" I asked.

"Nashua."

"What brought you up here?"

"I had enough of that life. I worked in a factory, all cooped up. The wife and I, we came up here three years ago. This is where a person can live."

"Where do you go when you want to go out at night?"

"I don't have to. I bought two VCRs, so I can copy the movies I rent. I've got four hundred movies up the house."

"Does your wife like it up here?" I asked.

"She'll be all right. She's had four nervous breakdowns."

We didn't catch any fish. Before noon, the sky darkened, and at the first sign of an electrical storm we took the aluminum boat in to shore. I paid the guide the price of a couple of movie rentals, and—with nothing else to do—drove north on Route 3, past the Second Connecticut Lake, and the Third. Both sides of the road were forest. On the other side of the border there were fields, a town and a jolly little bar with French music playing. I finished my beer and turned around, to where New Hampshire begins.

# For Further Reading

*Amoskeag: Life and Work in an American Factory City.* By Tamara K. Hareven and Randolph Langenbach. New York: Pantheon, 1978.

*The Great White Hills of New Hampshire.* By Ernest Poole. Garden City, New York: Doubleday, 1946.

*Let Me Show You New Hampshire.* By Ella Shannon Bowles. New York: Alfred A. Knopf, 1938.

*Lucy Crawford's History of the White Mountains.* Edited by Stearns Morse. Boston: Appalachian Mountain Club, 1978.

*Mount Washington: A Guide and Short History.* By Peter Randall. Camden, Maine: Down East Books, 1983.

*New Hampshire Beautiful.* By Wallace Nutting. Framingham, Massachusetts: Old America Publishers, 1923.

*New Hampshire: A Bicentennial History.* By Elizabeth Forbes Morison and Elting E. Morison. New York: Norton, 1976.

*New Hampshire: An Epitome of Popular Government.* By Frank B. Sanborn. Boston: Houghton Mifflin, 1904.

*New Hampshire Folk Tales.* By Eva A. Speare. Canaan, NH: Phoenix Publishing, 1974. (Original edition 1945).

*New Hampshire: A Guide to the Granite State.* Written by Workers of the Federal Writers Project of the Works Progress Administration for the State of New Hampshire. (American Guide Series.) Boston: Houghton Mifflin/The Riverside Press, 1938.

*New Hampshire: An Illustrated History of the Granite State.* By Ronald Jager and Grace Jager. Woodland Hills, California: Windsor Publishing Co., 1983.

*Roadside Geology of Vermont and New Hampshire.* By Bradford B. Van Diver. Missoula, Montana: Mountain Press, 1987.

*The White Hills: Their Legends, Landscape and Poetry.* By Thomas Starr King. Boston: Estes and Lauriat, 1887.

# AMERICAN GEOGRAPHIC PUBLISHING

**EACH BOOK HAS ABOUT 100 PAGES, 11" X 8½", 120 TO 170 COLOR PHOTO-GRAPHS**

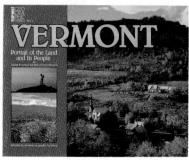

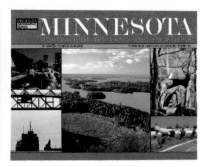

# Enjoy, See, Understand America State by State

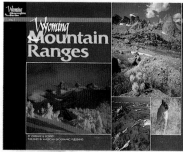

**American Geographic Publishing
Geographic Series of the States**

Lively, colorful, beautifully illustrated books specially written for these series explain land form, animals and plants, economy, lifestyle and history of each state or feature. Generous color photography brings each state to life and makes each book a treat to turn to frequently. The geographic series format is designed to give you more information than coffee-table photo books, yet so much more color photography than simple guide books.

**Each book includes:**
- Colorful maps
- Valuable descriptions and charts of features such as volcanoes and glaciers
- Up-to-date understanding of environmental problems where man and nature are in conflict
- References for additional reading, agencies and offices to contact for more information
- Special sections portraying people in their homes, at work, in the countryside

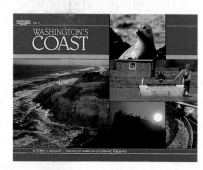

for more information write:
**American Geographic Publishing
P.O. Box 5630
Helena, Montana 59604**